The Holy Mass

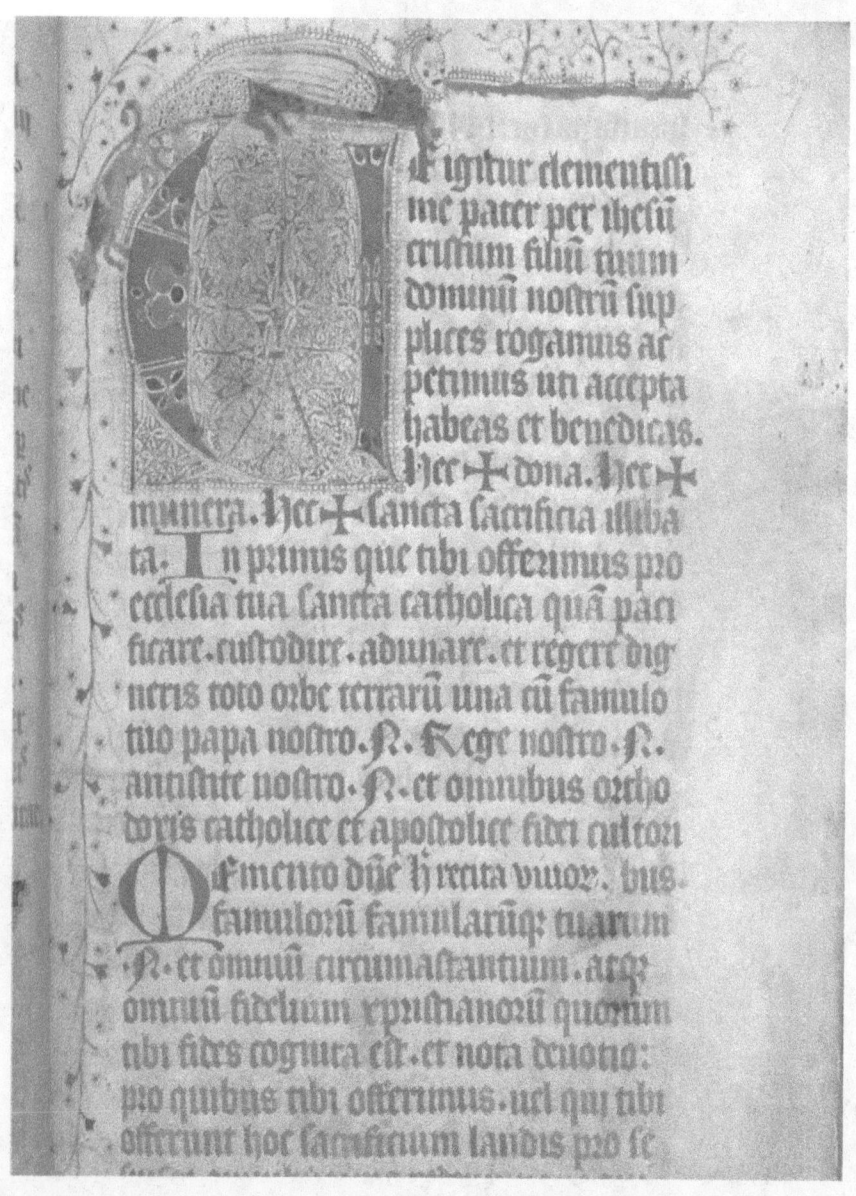

Canon page from a 13th century Benedictine Missal
British Library, 18031, 27r

THE HOLY MASS

The Eucharistic Sacrifice
and
The Roman Liturgy

Containing Volumes I and II

BY
THE REV. HERBERT LUCAS, S J.

MEDIATRIX PRESS

MMXVIII

ISBN: 978-1-953746-15-3

©Mediatrix Press, 2018, 2019.

The Holy Mass was originally printed by Manresa Press, London and is now in the Public Domain. Typesetting and layout of this edition is ©Mediatrix Press. No part of this edition may be reproduced electronically or physically except for reviews, or quotations in journals, blogs, or use in schools.

Nihil Obstat:

S. Georgius Kieran Hyland, S.t.d.,
Censor Deputatus

Imprimatur:
✠ Petrus Epûs Southwarc.

Cover art:
The Mass of St. Gregory
Diego de la Cruz

Mediatrix Press
607 E. 6th Ave.
Post Falls, ID 83854
www.mediatrixpress.com

Table of Contents

THE HOLY MASS VOL. I

Prefatory Note ix

CHAPTER I
    Sacrifice and Sacrament. 1

CHAPTER II
    The Christian Altar and the Heavenly Sanctuary . . 11

CHAPTER III
    Priest, Prophet and King; the Parts of the Mass 19

CHAPTER IV
    The Roman Missal and its Ancestry. 25

CHAPTER V
    The Liturgy: High Mass and Low Mass: Survivals and Accretions 37

CHAPTER VI
    The Collect, Secreta and Postcommunion. 53

CHAPTER VII
    The Lessons from Holy Scripture. 63

CHAPTER VIII
    The Offertory 75

THE HOLY MASS VOL. II.

Prefatory Note. 93

CHAPTER IX
    The Preface. 95

CHAPTER X
    The Canon —I. 107

CHAPTER XI
    The Canon - II 119

CHAPTER XII
    The Canon - III. 127

CHAPTER XIII
    The Canon - IV. 141

CHAPTER XIV
    The Pater Noster, the Fraction, and the Communion
    149

CHAPTER XV
    The Saints and the Mass 163

CHAPTER XVI
    The Roman and Early Gallican Rites. 169

PREFATORY NOTE

THE attempt to write yet another book about the Mass, while, for English-speaking Catholics, Dr. Fortescue's work on the Roman Liturgy holds the field, may be deemed, perchance, both presumptuous and inopportune. It has been thought, however, that there is room for a shorter and more popular treatment of the same subject, and I have been asked to undertake it. The following pages will, however, be found to contain no mere summary of Dr. Fortescue's more erudite and comprehensive treatise. Indeed, as will appear more particularly in Chapters X—XIII and XVI, the opinions here put forward on more than one question of some importance will be found to differ from those to which that distinguished scholar has given expression. A considerable portion of the contents of these two little volumes has, in substance, already appeared in print, in the form of articles contributed to The Dublin Review (1893—4), The Tablet (1896, &c.). The Month (1900 and 1902), and lastly to a couple of local magazines, viz. *The Xaverian* and *The Ignatian Record* (1908—10).

The matter of these articles has, however, been thoroughly revised and for the most part recast; and in the process sundry views which the writer had formerly held have been notably modified. It only remains for me to thank the Editors or former Editors of the above-named reviews and periodicals for permission to reproduce, as far as might be deemed advisable, the contributions in question.

Herbert Lucas, S.J.
St. Francis Xavier's,
Liverpool,
January, 1914.

HOLY MASS
VOL. I

THE EUCHARISTIC SACRIFICE
AND
THE ROMAN LITURGY

CHAPTER I
SACRIFICE AND SACRAMENT

N the Catechism of Christian Doctrine which is in use in our Catholic schools, and which is familiar to all of us, after a dozen or so of questions and answers concerning the Sacrament of the Holy Eucharist, we come to the words: "Is the Holy Eucharist a Sacrament only? No ... it is also a Sacrifice"; words which, to a hyper-critical reader might almost suggest the thought that the Holy Sacrifice of the Mass should be regarded as in a manner subsidiary to the Sacrament of our Lord's Body and Blood. This, of course, is by no means the case. In dealing with the Sacrament before touching on the doctrine of the Church regarding the Mass, the compilers of our catechism have wisely followed the example set by the Fathers of the Council of Trent, both in their preliminary discussions, and also in the final reduction of the conciliar decrees and canons. And indeed the reasons which led them to adopt this course are not far to seek. For, until the dogmas of the Real Presence and of Transubstantiation have been established, it is plainly impossible to make good the sacrificial character of the Eucharist. In the words of our own Bishops: "If there were no power in the word of consecration to make the true body and blood of Christ really and objectively present,... we should not have on our altars the Victim of Calvary, and without its Victim the sacrifice could not subsist."[1] Nevertheless, it is worthy of remark that logically, and one may even say historically, the

---

[1] "Vindication of the Bull on Anglican Orders," p. 12.

Eucharistic Sacrifice is prior to the Sacrament, since the reception of the latter is essentially a participation in the former, and pertains to its integrity. The Sacrament, as received by the faithful in Holy Communion, is the fruit of the Sacrifice. It is not merely the Body and Blood of our Lord, together with His human Soul and His Divinity, which we receive, but His Body and Blood under the special aspect of a Victim which has been sacrificially offered. And this is a point on which it seems desirable to lay some stress, not merely on the general ground that every object of human knowledge gains in clearness by being looked at from various points of view, but also for a reason peculiar to the matter in hand. For it is incontestable that the sacrificial system of the Old Law, pointing as it does to the existence of some kind of eucharistic sacrifice under the New Dispensation, suggests considerations which are well calculated to predispose the mind of an enquirer after the truth towards the Catholic doctrine concerning the Sacrament of the Eucharist, apart from which, as has been said, the Eucharistic Sacrifice "could not," in fact, "subsist."

It would be superfluous and inopportune to enter here upon a discussion as to the origin of sacrifice, and as to the precise significance of its primitive forms. Whatever may be the true answer to the question whether the idea of sacrifice has its ultimate roots in a natural instinct or in a primitive revelation, or whether, as is perhaps more probable, revelation came to the aid of instinct, to guide it and keep it in check, it may, at any rate, safely be said that the Sacrifice of the New Dispensation should be considered as immediately and designedly related rather to the fully developed system which it was to supplant, than to the more rudimentary institutions of remoter times. Whatever may have been the case in prehistoric ages, or among barbarous peoples, it is plain that in the levitical code the idea which lies at the root of all sacrifice is that of an offering, of an offering which affords a means of access to God, of an offering which is in some sense vicarious, as symbolical of the self-oblation of the offerer. To state the matter as briefly as possible, the notion of sacrifice and of self-sacrifice are indissolubly connected, even though the connection may often have been obscured, or forgotten, or overlooked.

Now this oblation, or self-oblation, might have three several ends or purposes. It might be a simple and yet most solemn acknowledgment of the supreme dominion of God; and this would seem to have been the true inward significance of the holocaust or whole-burnt offering. Or it might be in the nature of a thank- offering or peace-offering, terms which sufficiently explain themselves. Or again it might have for its specific purpose the removal of an obstacle, in the form of a sin or trespass, which impeded the approach of the offender to God; in which case the sacrifice would be in the strict sense propitiatory. This threefold division of sacrifices according to their moral character or purpose is, it need hardly be said, explicitly and repeatedly recognized in Holy Scripture; and the order of enumeration, corresponding as it does to descending grades of dignity, is that which is followed in the opening chapters of the Book of Leviticus, where the subject is systematically dealt with. But the normal order of actual succession was necessarily different from this.

It is plain that for the attainment of the end ultimately desired, viz., full fellowship with God, it was needful that obstacles should first be removed; and accordingly, in the actual carrying out of the ritual, the sin-offering or the trespass-offering took precedence of the other kinds of sacrifice.[2] After the sin-offering, the holocaust; and then, to put the seal—as it were—upon the reconciliation already effected, came the thank-offering or peace-offering.[3]

It is next to be observed that there were certain characteristic details which differentiated these three kinds of sacrificial oblation, and which have an important bearing on

---

[2] E.g. Lev. 16:3.

[3] Lev. 9:8, 12, 18.

the manifold significance of the unique and all-consummating Sacrifice of the New Law. That in the holocaust or whole-burnt offering the entire victim was consumed by fire on the altar, is sufficiently indicated by the terms employed to describe this species of sacrificial oblation in the Septuagint and in the Vulgate, as well as in the English versions, Catholic and Anglican. It is less clearly implied in the original Hebrew word ʿolah, which means a "sending up" or "causing to ascend." In the sacrifice for sin, a portion only of the victim was laid upon the altar, the remainder—when the ritual was carried out with full solemnity—being taken "outside the camp" to be there burnt as a thing unhallowed.[4] On these more solemn occasions at least, no portion of the victim might be eaten, either by the offerer or by the priest. It was only in the case of private and particular sin-offerings that the priests had their allotted portion reserved to them;[5] and this allowance must be taken to have been something of a derogation from the fuller symbolism of the more solemn ritual. The rite of the peace-offering was of a widely different character. Here the sacrificial meal was of primary importance. A portion of the victim was consumed by fire, a second portion was reserved for the priest or priests, but the greater part of the flesh was eaten by the offerer and his friends, special mention being made in the 22nd Psalm of the poor as guests at the feast.[6]

Now in a sentence which has been embodied in one of the prayers in the Roman Missal (the "Secreta" of the seventh Sunday after Pentecost), St. Leo tells us that in His one sacrifice Our Lord has united and consummated the ancient rites with all their diversities. The words, which like every other good example of ecclesiastical Latin suffer in the process of translation, are these: "Deus, qui legalium differentiam

---

[4] 16:27.

[5] Lev. 6:18.

[6] Lev. 7:15; 19:6; Ps. 22[23]:27.

hostiarum unius sacrificii perfectione sanxisti; accipe sacrificium," &c. And indeed it is easy to see that Christ's offering of Himself was a holocaust by reason of its completeness, a propitiatory offering for sin by reason of its atoning efficacy and purpose, and finally a peace-offering whereby the atonement was not only made but sealed by a sacrificial meal.

That the Sacrifice of Calvary had the character of a holocaust is not indeed asserted in express terms anywhere in the New Testament; but it is very clearly implied in the Epistle to the Hebrews, where the perfection of our Lord's self-offering is contrasted with the imperfections of the ancient sacrifices, the holocaust being included in the brief enumeration.[7] More explicitly the writer of the same Epistle calls attention to the fact that Christ suffered "extra portam"—"outside the gate," thus carrying out in His own person the symbolism of the sin-offering, in which (as has been said) the body of the victim was burnt "extra castra"—"outside the camp."[8] And he develops at considerable length the antitypal relation of the sacrifice of the Cross with that most solemn of all the expiatory sacrifices of the Old Law which was offered on the day of Atonement.[9] Here, however, it will be well briefly to forestall a possible objection. It may be said that precisely in so far as Our Lord, by suffering "extra portam," fulfilled the special symbolism of the sin-offering, He departed from that of the holocaust. But the answer is easy, and ought to satisfy anyone but the most captious.

While from a merely human point of view Our Lord suffered as an outcast far from the temple precincts, yet His own body was the veritable temple or tabernacle of which the sacred edifice on Sion was but the type. "I banish you," says

---

[7] Hebr. 10, sqq.

[8] Hebr. 13:12 sq.

[9] Hebr. 9:6 sq.

Coriolanus in the play, to the Roman Senators; and the Synagogue which spurned and rejected the Messiah was itself rejected of God. Where Christ was, there was the legitimate tabernacle and altar, and so the characteristic features of the holocaust were not wanting to His self-offering.

But it was essential to the antitypal perfection of this all-sufficing sacrifice that it should likewise include the specific qualities of a peace-offering; and these it can be said to have possessed only if the Holy Eucharist be taken into account. As in the peace-offerings of the Old Law the flesh of the victim was no less truly eaten than the victim itself was truly slain, so also—but after a more perfect manner—it must needs be in the case of the supremely perfect sacrifice of the New Dispensation. In the ancient rite, conditioned as it was by the limitations of material objects, only a portion of the victim could be offered on the altar, since a portion was to be eaten. Here the whole is offered and the whole is eaten. Moreover, the whole is eaten entire by every one of the faithful, in accordance with the words of St. Thomas's hymn:

> Sic totum omnibus, quod totum singulis;
> "So giveth He all to all that He giveth all to each."

And again:

> Sumit unus, sumunt mille,
> Tantum isti quantum ille,
> Nec sumptus consumitur.

Which may be rendered thus:

> Taketh one or take Him many
> Each hath much as all, nor any
> Can consume what all may eat.

But there is another point of correspondence to be noted. The sacrifices of the Old Law were divided, as regards the nature of the objects offered, into two classes, viz., those in which the blood of a living victim was shed, and the bloodless offerings of meal and wine. It must however be borne in mind that these two kinds of "oblata" were not *per se* mutually independent, but that the second class was supplementary to the first. In the 15th chapter of the Book of Numbers it is clearly laid down that for every animal victim that was immolated a certain measure of meal and of wine was likewise to be offered.

It is also prescribed in the second chapter of Leviticus, that when an offering of meal was made, the priest was to lay a handful of the meal upon the altar "as a memorial."[10] The precise significance of this phrase is, indeed, extremely obscure; but bearing in mind the typological nature of the sacrifices of the Old Law, we should be led to expect, under the New Dispensation, (1) that there would be a bloodless offering supplementary to the great Sacrifice of Calvary, and (2) that, in some way or other, this bloodless offering would have the character of "a memorial." How fully this antecedent expectation is fulfilled in the Holy Eucharist it is hardly necessary to point out. The Sacrifice of the Mass is supplementary to the Sacrifice of the Cross—in substance one with it, in act distinct from it—and it is, as our Lord Himself has told us, in the nature of a "memorial."

What has already been said will, it is hoped, have helped the reader to appreciate, in their special bearing on the Holy Eucharist, the force of St. Paul's assertion that the sacrifices of the Old Law were no more than "a shadow," and yet so far as they went a truthful shadow, "of good things" that were "to come"; and of his more definite assertion that "we have an altar whereof they have no power to eat, who"—after the final setting aside of the Old Dispensation—continue to "serve the tabernacle" of the levitical ordinances, preferring the shadowy type to the glorious reality.[11]

How immeasurably this glorious reality does indeed

---

[10] Lev. 2:2.

[11] Hebr. 10:1; 13:10. The Pauline authorship, in substance it not as regards the very words, of the Epistle to the Hebrews is here assumed.

surpass its shadowy types may in some degree be understood from the following considerations. With certain exceptions, to be found in the case of a sacrificial offering made by a priest on his own behalf, every sacrifice for which provision is made in the levitical ordinances, may be said to have involved a two-fold substitution; the substitution on the one hand of the priest, and on the other hand of the victim, for the person on whose behalf the sacrifice was offered. And on both counts these sacrifices were not merely imperfect, but of their very nature essentially and intrinsically inadequate. They were in the first place imperfect because the priest who offered them, even though he had been ceremonially set apart from his fellow-men for this very purpose and thereby invested with a kind of official sanctity, was, nevertheless, like his fellow-men, a sinner; and he was, therefore, in his personal capacity, unsuited to act as a mediator on their behalf. "For every high priest taken from among men is ordained for men in (or, unto) the things that appertain to God, that he may offer up gifts and sacrifices for sins; who can have compassion on them that are ignorant and that err, because he himself also is compassed with infirmity; and therefore he ought, as for the people, so also for himself, to offer for sins."[12]

The levitical sacrifices were, in the second place, essentially imperfect and inadequate because the animals which were offered as a substitute for him who offered them, were of no intrinsic value in the sight of God. "If you should kindle the forests of a whole mountain side," He says in effect, "and consume in one great holocaust all the beasts that dwell therein, it would be of no account in My eyes." "And Lebanon shall not be enough to burn, nor the beasts thereof sufficient for a burnt offering."[13] The substitution of a dumb animal for a man was a purely symbolic rite, having precisely the value of

---

[12] Hebr. 5:1-3.

[13] Isaiah 40:16.

a symbol and no more. And the willingness of the victim to be thus offered by way of sacrifice, though crudely represented or simulated by means of garlands or stately trappings, was, after all, a mere legal fiction. But in the sacrifice of Calvary—perpetuated in the Mass—our great High Priest, Christ Jesus our Lord, was and is of unique dignity and of unique aptness for His office. For He possessed and possesses both the nature of God who was to be propitiated, and the nature of man on whose behalf the propitiation was to be made. It is in this sense that He was the ideally perfect Mediator, the "one Mediator," by means of an all-sufficient oblation, between man and God.[14] For the Victim again, was of infinite price; and besides this, since Priest and Victim were one, there was in this case no mere symbolical substitution of an unwilling animal for a being of a higher order, but an entirely voluntary self-substitution of the infinitely worthy for the graceless sinner.

Another reflection may fitly find expression here. It is one which, though it more immediately concerns such as are in priestly orders, has its application to the laity also, and it may be usefully called to mind as often as we say or hear Mass.[15] The grace of ordination to the priesthood not only confers the power of consecrating the sacred elements, and so of offering—in union with our Lord—the bloodless sacrifice of His Body and Blood; but it also stimulates or should stimulate the priest to make a complete and unreserved self-offering, in union with the self-offering of Christ whose priesthood he shares. As Christ was both Priest and Victim, so should the members of His priesthood be. Nor is this a new-fangled or farfetched notion. Every Christian altar, as we know, has the character of a tomb or sepulchre, inasmuch as it contains enshrined within it or beneath it, the relics of martyrs, in accordance with those words of the Apocalypse: "I saw beneath

---

[14] Tim. 2:5. Cf. Hebr. 8:6; 9:15; 12:24.

[15] Cf. Lucas, *At the Parting of the Ways,* pp. 238 ff.

the altar [in heaven] the souls of them that were slain for the Word of God and for the testimony which they held."[16] The usage, and the hallowed words on which it is founded, alike remind us that the sufferings of the martyrs are incorporated as it were and made one with the sufferings of Christ, and that, in virtue of this incorporation, they are accepted by God as a true and efficacious sacrifice.

Nor, as has been said, is this a matter which concerns priests alone. The whole body of the faithful, in virtue of their vital union with Christ our Lord, may be regarded as in some sense participating in His priesthood, and all are or may be associated with Him in His function as a propitiatory victim. It was not to ecclesiastics alone, but to the faithful at large, that St. Paul wrote: "I beseech you, therefore, by the mercy of God, that you present your bodies a living sacrifice, holy, pleasing unto God, your reasonable service."[17] Instances of the Christian spirit of self-sacrifice among the laity abound, not only in the history of the Church at large, but in the unwritten records of the hidden life of the poor in every city and country of the world. May they abound yet more in the years that are to come. Nor is there any more efficacious means whereby this desirable consummation may be brought about than diligence in hearing Holy Mass as often as we can, and more especially by that fuller participation in the Holy Sacrifice which is afforded by frequent and—when possible—daily Communion.

---

[16] Apoc. 6:9.
[17] Rom. 12:1.

CHAPTER II
THE CHRISTIAN ALTAR AND THE HEAVENLY SANCTUARY

OME further observations on the sacrificial character of the Mass may usefully engage our attention before we proceed to consider the liturgy in detail.

In the great majority of theological treatises on the Holy Eucharist which have been published since the Council of Trent, it has been either asserted or assumed that the idea of sacrifice involves that of an offering made byway of "destruction." And since in the Holy Eucharist as such there is no physical "destruction," theologians have been greatly puzzled to explain how the definition of a "sacrifice" is verified in the Mass. Vasquez, for instance, who has had many followers, states the matter thus: "Since by the force of the words, only the Body of Christ is put under the species of bread, and only His Blood under the species of wine—although under either species the whole Christ is present by concomitance—the consecration of the two separate species thus performed constitutes a representation of that separation of the Body from the Blood which makes death; and this representation is called a mystical separation. And the death itself is represented; therefore it is called a mystical slaying. ... Before the consecration of the wine, the Body of Christ is not represented as dead or immolated." Lugo on the other hand, whose opinion has been popularized by more than one English writer, holds that the essential idea of sacrifice, as involving some kind of "destruction," is realized in a certain "exinanition" (or "kenosis" as a modem writer might say) which our Lord undergoes in placing Himself under the sacramental species. It is a self-abasement comparable with that of the Incarnation, and in some respects going even beyond it. For in the Holy Eucharist He lies as it were dead upon the altar, not so much by virtue of the mystical separation of the Blood from the Body of which Vasquez speaks, as by the fact that the natural operations and functions of the human body are suspended in the sacramental state. It is in this assumption of the "status victimae," or of a "status declivior," that, in this view, the element of destruction or quasi-destruction is to be found. According to Lugo and those who follow him, the double consecration is essential to the sacrifice, not as a matter of intrinsic necessity and *ex natura rei*, but simply as a matter of positive institution.

It is needless to proceed further in the enumeration of the various theories that have been devised to meet the difficulty. The very fact of their diversity is enough to show that no plea of universal acceptance can be set up on behalf of any one of them. Roughly speaking, they are all reducible—as has been already implied—to the statement that in the act of consecration there is some kind of "moral" or "equivalent" destruction, and that thus the "ratio sacrificii" is saved. But all such explanations leave it open to the objector to say: "If destruction is a necessary element in sacrifice, then where the destruction is real, there will be or may be a real sacrifice; but where the destruction is only 'moral' or 'symbolical' or 'equivalent' (which really means not quite equivalent) the rite, however solemn, will be a sacrifice only in some moral or symbolical or equivalent—or not quite equivalent—sense."

In our own days the suggestion has been made—and the point has been developed and insisted on by more than one distinguished theologian—that the whole of this difficulty has been occasioned by a misapprehension as to the precise part which "destruction" holds in the notion of sacrifice, or—to state the matter slightly otherwise—as to the part which destruction

Chapter II: Christian Altar and Heavenly Sanctuary

actually held in the sacrificial system of the Mosaic law. That animal victims offered in sacrifice must be slain is, of course, beyond dispute. Yet even in the case of animal victims it is particularly deserving of notice that the actual slaying of the victim was by no means the most important item in the ritual. Indeed, the act of slaying the victim was not *per se* a priestly function at all. It could be performed, and usually was performed, not by the priest, but by the person who made the offering. The priest's duty was to receive the victim's blood, to pour it about the altar, to lay upon the altar the body or a portion of the body, according to the nature of the sacrifice, and, of course, to kindle the fire by which it was to be consumed. The distinction between the part which was assigned to the offerer and that which was proper to the priest is quite clearly laid down at the outset of the Book of Leviticus; and it certainly should not be left out of account in any serious discussion of the subject. The case has been forcibly stated by Wilhelm and Scannell, in a passage which summarizes the teaching of Professor Schanz:

> The notion of offering (*oblatio, prosphora*) may be taken as the fundamental notion of all sacrifices.... The burning or out-pouring of the gifts hands them over to God, and through their acceptance God admits the giver to communion with Him. For the essential character of the sacrificial gift is not its destruction, but its handing over and consecration to God.... The out-pouring of the libation and the killing of the animals are but the means for handing over the gift to God, and for bringing the giver into communion with Him. The killing necessarily precedes the burning, but the killing is not the sacrifice. 'The victim is killed in order to be offered';[1] in other words the killing is preparatory to the sacrifice. More importance attaches to the blood of the victim which is gathered and poured out at the altar. For, according to ancient ideas, the life, or the soul, is in the blood. When, therefore, the blood is offered, the highest that man can give, viz., a soul or a life, is handed over to God.... [Again] the

---

[1] Greg. M. *in Ezech* I. 2, Hom. 10, 19.

sanctifying power of fire is as well known as the role it plays in heathen mythologies. God Himself was a fire, 'Our God is a consuming fire,'[2] or the fire was a power sent down from heaven, and frequently the heavenly fire is said to have consumed the victim. ... The independent unbloody sacrifices can only be explained from the same point of view, viz., that they express oblation of self to, and union with, God. ... Sacrifice in general may, therefore, be defined as 'the offering to God, by an authorized minister, of an actual gift of something of our own transformed by the consecration of the minister, and thus passing into the dominion of God, Who accepts the gift for the sanctification of the offerer.'[3]

To say, however, that the slaying of the victim is not the sacrificial act *par excellence* is a very different thing from saying (what would be altogether untrue) that the victim's death is not of the essence of sacrifice. The animal sacrifices of the Old Law were, as has already been said, an attempt to shadow forth the voluntary self-offering of a vicarious substitute. But as was also said, it is to be remembered that every sacrifice involved a double substitution, viz., that of the victim, and—under another aspect—that of the priest for the offerer. And it is only another way of expressing the same truth to say that the priest was in a very true sense a substitute for the victim. As victim, the animal represented the offerer. As presenter of the victim the priest performed on its behalf what by the nature of the case the victim could not (even had it been otherwise capable) have done for itself. Hence it is explicitly noted, as an element in the perfection of the sacrifice of Christ, that in this case Priest and Victim were one and the same. And yet even here the idea of substitution was not wanting, for here the all-perfect Victim was self-offered for his people. In the divine tragedy of Calvary it is plain that it was not the act of slaying our Lord that constituted the sacrifice, but our Lord's acceptance of the death

---

[2] Hebr. 12:29.

[3] Wilhelm and Scannel, *Dogmatic Theology* (1898), ii. 451.

Chapter II: Christian Altar and Heavenly Sanctuary

inflicted on Him. But it is also plain that the death was inflicted by those, or the representatives, on whose behalf the sacrifice was offered; so that in this respect also the typology was preserved or realized.

Although, however, in the case of a living victim, death by the shedding of blood was of the very essence of the sacrifice, inasmuch as it was a necessary and indispensable preliminary to the presentation of the flesh and the blood to God upon the altar, it is by no means clear that in the case of a commemorative sacrifice, in which, after the shedding of the blood "once for all," the same Victim is offered again and again, we are compelled to look for a repeated equivalent of the blood shedding, or for an element of real or equivalent "destruction." Under the limitations which conditioned the offering of animal victims, anything in the nature of a repetition of the offering was plainly impossible, even had there been reason for such repetition. But these limitations being absent in the case of the supreme sacrifice of Christ, it would seem that the sacrificial "presentation" or "oblation" of the Victim might be repeated indefinitely, and that nothing more was required in order to the realization of the idea of a true bloodless sacrifice than that the presentation or oblation should be made by means of a suitable outward and significant rite, not necessarily involving any sort of "destruction." That the rite actually chosen and instituted by our Lord does in fact "show forth His death" by virtue of the separate consecration of the host and of the chalice, is of course a truth to be maintained and cherished; and our attention is pointedly called to it by the words "mysterium fidei" ("the mystery of faith"), which are embodied in the form of consecration of the chalice. Nevertheless, in view of the divergence of opinions among theologians, it would seem to be desirable not to lay undue stress upon any of the particular explanations of the "ratio sacrificii" in the Mass, as though, if this particular explanation (*e.g.*, that of Vazquez or De Lugo) were mistaken, the "ratio sacrificii" would be lacking.

The point may be aptly illustrated by means of a comparison. In treating of the mystery of man's redemption two questions must be distinguished, viz.: 1) What was necessary in order that Christ our Lord might redeem mankind? and (2) how did our Lord in fact redeem mankind? To the first question the answer is that any single act of the God-Man would have been sufficient for the purpose. To the second the answer is that in fact our Lord redeemed us by dying on the cross. And to this simple statement may be added many considerations which bring into prominence the manifold congruity of the "plentiful redemption," going so far beyond the mere intrinsic necessities of the case, whereby we were redeemed.

Precisely so in dealing with the Sacrifice of the Mass we must distinguish between two questions, viz.: (1) What were the necessary and sufficient conditions to be fulfilled in order that the Mass might be a true sacrifice? and (2) what is it that in fact makes the Mass a true sacrifice? The first question has reference to the intrinsic necessities of the case, the second concerns the actual institution of the Eucharistic Sacrifice. To the first question it should, I think, be answered that—so far as we can see—any rite which God might have chosen to institute, whereby the Divine Victim, once slain, should be again self-offered upon an altar, would have been sufficient for the verification or realization of the "ratio sacrificii." For instance, it was not—so far as we can see—intrinsically impossible that there should have been a eucharistic sacrifice "under one kind," had it pleased God so to ordain; and it is at least exceedingly doubtful whether we are justified in postulating any second "destruction" or "quasi-destruction" or "mystical destruction" of the Victim, once slain, as an indispensable element in the rite. But to the second question the answer must be that, at least *de facto*, at least as a matter of positive divine ordinance, the particular rite whereby it has pleased our Lord to offer Himself again upon the Christian altar, and therefore the particular act by virtue of which the Holy Eucharist is a true sacrifice, consists in the double or separate consecration. And here again it is easy to point out the manifold congruity of the divine choice. So, too, the view he had taken leaves quite untouched the opinion of Lugo, in so far as this opinion has reference to the congruity of the actual form of the Eucharistic oblation rather than to its very essence. And thus the teaching of Vazquez and Lugo, instead of being opposed to one another, become mutually complementary, each emphasizing an important aspect of a many-sided truth. But it is important, as it seems to me, to avoid creating a gratuitous difficulty by laying down, as though it could be proved *a priori,* that what God has in fact done it was intrinsically necessary that He should do in order that the Mass might be a true sacrifice.

By way of supplementing and completing what has already been said, it may be useful to return for a moment to the relation which the death of the victim held to the completed sacrificial ritual. The death was necessary, not merely that the physical acts of pouring out the blood and burning the flesh might be accomplished, but that the very life of the victim, conceived of as being contained in the blood, might be removed, as it were, to another sphere of existence. Not, of course, that the soul of an animal could really survive its immolation. But this was precisely one of those many limitations by reason of which the sacrifices of the Old Law were mere types and symbols. The symbolical presentation of the animal's life—conceived as still contained in the blood—to God, was a faint foreshadowing of the act whereby our Lord, triumphant over death, offered or presented on our behalf the life which He had laid down yet not lost. It is particularly noteworthy that both in the Apocalypse and in the Epistle to the Hebrews the sacrifice of Christ is regarded as in a manner perennial and continuous, at least so far as regards the ritual act of the self-presentation of the Divine Victim. Christ having died on the Cross entered into the heavenly sanctuary to offer or present on our behalf, not the blood of goats and heifers, but His own.⁴ And he entered that heavenly sanctuary, not—like the levitical High Priest—to withdraw after a few moments, but to make everlasting intercession for us.⁵ So, too, on the Apocalyptic altar the Lamb for ever stands "as it were slain," *i.e.*, bearing all the marks of death, yet ever living, a propitiatory Victim to the end of time.⁶ And what—according to our way of reckoning—takes place in heaven continuously or perennially, is reproduced on earth, not indeed continuously in any single place, but daily and hourly on ten thousand altars "from the rising of the sun even to its going down."⁷

---

⁴ Hebr. 9:12.
⁵ Hebr. 7:25.
⁶ Apoc. 5:6.
⁷ Mal. 1:11.

CHAPTER III
PRIEST, PROPHET AND KING; THE PARTS OF THE MASS

OMETHING has been said, in the foregoing chapters, of Holy Mass as a sacrifice, having for one of its chief fruits the Holy Sacrament of the Eucharist. But before entering into an examination of the details of the liturgy, that is to say, of the lessons, the psalmody, the prayers, and the ceremonies in which the central act of sacrifice is enshrined, it may be worth while to take account of a truth that is too often overlooked, viz., that in the Mass, as it is actually celebrated all the world over, and not in the Roman rite alone, our Lord exercises, through His ministers, a threefold function, even as he exercised a threefold function in His visible human life on earth. He came, as we all know, in the character (1) of the supremely great Prophet or Teacher, (2) of the supremely perfect High Priest of the New Dispensation, and (3) of the King whose royalty was not of this world but who was to found and rule over an everlasting kingdom which is to have its final consummation in heaven. As Prophet, as God made Man that He might become His own messenger to mankind, He claims our faith. As our High Priest He laid, by His all-atoning sacrifice, the foundations of our hope. As King He appeals to our loyalty and love. Now to this threefold function of Christ our Lord correspond the three main portions into which the sacred liturgy of the Mass, apart from preliminaries and supplementary accretions, is divided.

The first portion, the "Missa catechumenorum," as it was once called, which corresponds with the teaching office of our Lord, consists, chiefly, though not exclusively, of lessons from Holy Scripture, followed, in the case of the principal parochial

Mass on Sundays, by a homily on the Gospel of the day, and, at all Masses on Sundays and on certain other days, by the chanting or recitation of the "Credo." It is plain that an appeal is here made primarily to our faith, a point which it is well to bear in mind, whatever "method of hearing Mass" we may adopt. Or, to express the same truth in a different form, our Lord in Holy Mass feeds us with the bread of the word before feeding us with His Body in the Holy Sacrament. A recent writer has indeed laid stress, undue stress, as it seems to me, on the fact—assuming it to be a fact—that this first portion of the Mass had its origin in a religious service distinct from the Holy Sacrifice. Now, that from the earliest times, doctrinal and catechetical services have been held apart from the Mass, and that these services did in fact take a form similar or at least analogous to that of the "Missa catechumenorum," inasmuch as they embodied the reading of passages from Holy Scripture, alternating with psalmody and prayer and followed by a homily, need not be called into question. Instances may be found in the "Peregrinatio Silviae" (or "Etheriae"), a very notable pilgrim-book of the fourth century; and indeed they may be found nearer home in the Matins and Lauds of the Divine Office. But with the exception of that apostolic age during which the Holy Sacrifice was immediately preceded by the Agape, without perhaps, the interposition of any reading or homily, it may be doubted whether any instance can be found of the celebration of Mass apart from an introductory doctrinal exordium.[1] The catechumens were excluded from being present at the "Missa fidelium"; but the faithful were expected, or they still are, to attend the "Missa catechumenorum" which preceded it.

That the second great division of the Mass, which embraces

---

[1] *Cf.* Cabrol, *Origines Liturgiques,* pp. 333 ff. The truth of the statement made above is not, as it seems to me, affected by the circumstance that the Mass might be commenced in one church (where the lessons were read) and, after a procession, continued and finished in another.

the offertory, preface and Canon, constitutes the specifically sacrificial portion of the service, is a statement which might seem to need neither proof nor illustration. At any rate, whatever it does need under either head, will be set forth later. The point on which I wish to insist at present is the relation of this central portion of liturgy to the virtue of hope. More than once in the epistle to the Hebrews St. Paul insists on the truth that our hopes of life everlasting rest entirely on the sacrifice offered by Christ our Lord. He speaks of "the hope set before us, which we have as an anchor of the soul, sure and firm, and which entereth in, even within the veil, where the fore-runner Jesus is entered for us, being made a High Priest forever according to the order of Melchisedech."[2] He tells us that our Lord "hath an everlasting priesthood whereby He is able also to save forever them that come to God by Him";[3] that He is "the Mediator of a better testament" than that which was given to Moses, "which is established on better promises";[4] that "Jesus is not entered into the Holies," *i.e.* a sanctuary "made with hands, ... but into heaven itself, that He may appear now in the presence of God for us";[5] and lastly that "we have a confidence in the entering into the Holies," that is to say, a sure hope that we shall, if we be faithful to God's law, enter into the heavenly sanctuary, "by the Blood of Christ," who has opened for us "a new and living way," being "a High Priest over the house of God."[6] Of course I am well aware of the objection that may be raised by non-Catholics against the appeal, in this connection, to the passages which have just been quoted, inasmuch as all of them have reference, primarily, to the Sacrifice of Calvary. For the purpose of the present chapter, however, it is assumed that

---

[2] Hebr. 6:18-20.

[3] Hebr. 7:24, 25.

[4] Hebr. 8:6.

[5] Hebr. 9:24.

[6] Hebr. 10:19-21.

the Eucharistic sacrifice is a perpetuation of the sacrifice offered on the Cross, and that what is said of the efficacy of the one is, by consequence, true also of the other.

It can hardly be doubted that the hearing of Mass will more efficaciously help to strengthen the tempted and console the afflicted if due attention is paid to this intimate and special connection of the Holy Sacrifice, as such, with the virtue of hope, than if it were overlooked. By the words "Sursum Corda," and by the prayers, "Communicantes" and "Nobis quoque peccatoribus," we are not only bidden to lift our hearts above earthly cares and vanities, but reminded that our fellowship is with the saints who are gone before us, and that our true franchise (our "conversation" as the Douay Version has it) is in heaven.[7] And this in virtue of that very sacrifice-one with that of the Cross—at which we are assisting. The hearing of Mass should be to us as a vision of the true Jacob's ladder, reaching from earth to heaven, the ascent of which has been made possible for us solely by the merits of Christ's Precious Blood shed for us on Calvary, and through all time offered for us on the Christian altar.

If the Mass of the Catechumens appeals to our faith, and the prayers and ceremonies which more immediately accompany the act of sacrifice are calculated and intended to keep alive and reawaken our hopes of eternal life, it is plain enough that the concluding portion of the Mass, of which Holy Communion, received either sacramentally or spiritually, either personally or (so to say) vicariously, is the essential element, has a no less specific relation to the virtue and disposition of charity or love. This is so palpably evident that there is no need to labor the point.

It is, however, not so obviously plain that charity has a special relation with the kingly office of our Lord. Yet that this is so there can, I believe, be no reasonable doubt. The love which is demanded of us is not, primarily, affective but

---

[7] Phil. 3:20.

effective; its seat is not in the feelings or emotions but in the will; not sentiment but loyalty is the tribute that is due from us; and it is a tribute due to our Divine Saviour as our Sovereign Lord and Master. "If you love Me, keep My commandments,"[8] He says; and if the lowest and most indispensable kind of charity consists in obedience, the highest manifestations of the love of Christ are those of the Saints who, with a more generous loyalty, have followed more closely in His footsteps, fighting under His Standard of the Cross, and rejoicing to suffer with Him. So much for charity, or the love of our Lord, in general. As regards the Holy Eucharist in particular, it is as a King that Christ, the Bridegroom, woos His Bride, the Chinch, the Holy Eucharist is the chief pledge of his love, and Holy Communion is "the marriage-feast of the King's Son,"[9] or rather, perhaps, a foretaste of that marriage-feast in its full consummation.[10] It is, in the same inchoate sense, "the marriage-feast of the Lamb,"[11] of "the Lamb that was slain"[12] and yet liveth forever and "whose name is King of kings and Lord of Lords."[13] "Blessed are they that are called to the marriage-supper of the Lamb";[14] and it is well that we should know and recognize, even "as in a glass, darkly,"[15] the blessedness that is ours in this Sacrament of union and love.[16]

---

[8] St. John 14:15.

[9] St. Matth. 22:2 ff.

[10] Apoc. 9:7.

[11] Apoc. 19:7.

[12] Apoc. 5:6, 9, 12.

[13] Apoc. 17:14.

[14] Apoc. 19:9.

[15] 1 Cor. 13:12.

[16] For the leading ideas of this chapter I am indebted to reminiscences of certain sections in the fourth volume of Dr. Amberger's *Pastoral-Theologie*, a work which I have not been able to consult again at the time of writing.

CHAPTER IV
THE ROMAN MISSAL AND ITS ANCESTRY

T may be useful to state, at the outset of the present chapter, that the terms "Mass," "the Mass," or "a Mass," must here be understood as having reference to the verbal or printed text of the liturgical service, and not primarily to the great sacrificial act of which the verbal or printed text is but the outward vesture. Looking at the text as a whole, it is found to consist, mainly, of (1) Prayers, (2) lessons from Holy Scripture, and (3) choral pieces. Of the Scripture lessons and the choral pieces it will not be necessary to say anything in detail just at present. But of the prayers this much at least must here be noted, viz.: That they are either (1) fixed or (2) variable: that the fixed prayers are those which belong to *(a)* the "Ordinary" and *(b)* the "Canon" of the Mass (though the Canon allows of certain minor variations on the Festivals, and during the Octaves of Christmas, Epiphany, Easter, Ascension Day and Pentecost); that, of these two portions, the Canon, which extends from the end of the Preface to the *Pater Noster* exclusively, is thoroughly Roman in structure and composition, while the prayers which make up the bulk of the Ordinary are of later introduction, and are probably in large measure of Gallican origin or provenance; and lastly, that the variable prayers are the Collect, the Secreta, and the Post-Communion (with, on occasion, the "Oratio super populum"), which vary from day to day, and the Preface, which, roughly speaking, varies with the season.

Now the Roman Missal, by which for present purposes must be understood the official "Missale Romanum" with its authentic supplements, as distinct from sundry abridged and adapted translations thereof, contains the full text of all the Masses which must or may be sung or said on every day of the year. I say "which must or may be sung or said," because there are days on which a certain liberty of choice is allowed. For instance, on minor festival days occurring during Lent, the celebrant has the option of saying either the Mass of the feast or that of the feria; and there are many occasions, in the course of the year, on which "votive" Masses (e.g., a Mass for the deceased) may be celebrated. Of the Roman Missal it may be truthfully said that it derives its descent from the particular copy of St. Gregory's Mass-book which, at the Emperor's own request, Pope Hadrian I sent to Charlemagne, to serve as a guide and pattern for the liturgical usage of all the churches in his dominions. And it is to this origin that we owe the indications, in Missals intended for use all the world over, of the local Roman "Stations," of which something must be said hereafter.

It would, however, be a mistake to imagine that nothing more is needed except the omission from the Roman Missals of the prayers, lessons and antiphons proper to festivals of later origin, in order to get back to St. Gregory's Mass-book. And this for the simple reason that St. Gregory's Mass-book was not, strictly speaking, a "Missal." The Missal as we know it has, in fact, arisen out of the fusion of some four or five distinct books. In the days when all books were in manuscript, and liturgical books usually or commonly engrossed on parchment, it is easy to understand that economy in material and in labor was an all-important consideration. The Mass, so far as the words and ceremonies were concerned, was a highly dramatic service, in which the celebrant, the deacon, the sub-deacon, and the choir or "schola cantorum," each had their appointed parts; and it was obviously reasonable that each should have a book containing only the portion of the service which pertained to himself. The celebrant, in primitive times and in the early

Middle Ages, did not himself read the Epistle and the Gospel, or the choral parts of the Mass; and accordingly his book—the "Sacramentarium" as it was called—did not contain these. Its contents consisted of the Canon (for the "Ordinary" was of later introduction), together with the variable prayers (collects, *secretae*, and postcommunions) and the prefaces, with, it may be added, an appendix of sundry forms of blessing, etc. The deacon's book, the "Evangeliarium," contained Gospels only, and the subdeacon in like manner had his Lectionary, unless, indeed, as would often be the case, the lessons were read from a Bible or New Testament, or from a volume containing some portions thereof. For, as is well known, marginal notes, indicating the commencement and end of the liturgical lessons, are found in many early Biblical MSS. So too, the cantors and the choir had the book or books which, under the various names of "Antiphonarium," "Graduate," "Cantatorium," contained, set to musical notation, the choral portions of the Mass, *i.e.*, introits, graduals, tracts and sequences, and the antiphons at the offertory and Communion. "Antiphonarium," it may be observed, is a more comprehensive term than "Graduale" or "Gradale." In Rome the Graduate was called "Cantatorium."[1]

This at any rate was the ideal, and no doubt in cathedrals and great abbey churches the normal usage. But it is hardly to be supposed that in the eighth and ninth centuries, for instance, every parish priest had in his possession a full set of liturgical books, and it is at least probable that many had to be content with a small manual more or less similar to the "Stowe Missal." This is an early Irish Mass-book which resembles our modern missals in that it contains the entire text of the liturgy, and not merely the celebrant's part, while on the other hand it contains only three Masses, one for ordinary use ("cottidiana"), one for Saints' days, and one for the dead.

To sum up the whole matter in a few words:—Our present

---

[1] Amalarius in *P.L.* cv. 1245; *Cath. Encycl.* I. 579.

usage, by which the celebrant reads the whole of the Mass, including the parts originally proper to deacon, sub-deacon and choir, as well as his own, must needs have had its origin in what is now known as a "Low Mass"—i.e., a Mass without deacon, subdeacon or choir; a form of celebration which necessarily presupposes the combination in a single volume of elements proper to the sacramentary, lectionary, and gradual respectively. This fusion naturally took place at first on a small scale and in a fragmentary fashion, as in the "Stowe Missal," and it reached its final stage of completeness for all churches, however obscure, only when the invention of printing had facilitated the multiplication of copies, and the enforcement, by pontifical decrees, of liturgical uniformity.

And now, let us turn to the Roman Missal itself, and examine its contents. Let it be supposed that the reader has in his hands a copy of the "Missale Romanum," such as ought to be in the hands of every one who can read and understand the simple yet stately Latin of the Church's liturgy.

The volume is divided into the following parts:

1. The "Proprium de Tempore" or Proper of the Season. This contains the Masses for all the Sundays in the year, beginning with Advent Sunday, for Ascension Day and Corpus Christi, and for the week-days in Lent, Easter-week and Whitsun-week, the Rogation days, and the Ember days occurring in September and December. It is in the nature of a survival from a more primitive arrangement that the Masses for the Christmas season, *i.e.*, from Christmas Eve till the Octave of the Epiphany, though determined by the day of the month and not by the day of the week, yet find a place in the "Proprium de Tempore." In other words this collocation of the Christmas festivals points back to a time when the "Sanctorale" (of which presently) had not been separated from the "Temporale."

The circumstance that the Ordinary and Canon of the

Chapter IV: The Roman Missal and Its Ancestry

Mass, with the variable prefaces, find their place, not as might have been expected at the beginning or at the end of the book, but immediately before the Mass for Easter Sunday, calls for a word of explanation. It has been suggested that this arrangement is really due to considerations of convenience, in as much as the book opens more easily in the middle. It seems to me, however, more likely that the position of the Canon in the Missal is not unconnected with the fact that the great festival of Easter was the nucleus from which the ecclesiastical calendar was developed. This, if I understand him rightly, is Ebner's opinion; but he points out that the practice varied in successive centuries. In the earliest extant MSS., from the seventh century down to the close of the eighth, the Canon is found near the end of the book, either as a separate item or, more frequently, embodied in a "Missa cottidiana" or Mass for days not specially provided for. But from the beginning of the ninth century it takes its place, more naturally as one would think, at the beginning of the book. Finally, in MSS. of the twelfth and thirteenth centuries, it gradually settled down, so to say, into its present position; a position which it probably owes to the special honour which was felt to be due to the central solemnity of Easter.[2] At any rate there can be no question as to the practical convenience of the present arrangement.

2. The "Proprium Sanctorum." This contains the Masses appointed for those festivals—chiefly Saints' days—which are determined by the civil calendar, *i.e.*, which are assigned to certain days of the successive months from November 27th, the earliest possible date for the first Sunday in Advent, to November 26th. It contains, in addition, the Masses for a few feasts of comparatively recent origin, which, like that of the Sacred Heart of Jesus, are determined by the days of the ecclesiastical and not of the civil calendar.

3. The "Commune Sanctorum." As a matter of convenience

---

[2] Ebner, *Quellen u. Forschungen*, usw. pp. 363-372.

certain Masses have been drawn up suitable for any saint of a particular class, Martyr Confessor, Virgin, &c., and it not unfrequently happens that the whole or part of the Mass for the festival of this or that individual servant of God is taken from the "Common of Saints," while in the case of others the whole of the variable portion of the Mass is "proper," that is to say, peculiar to their own feast.

4. The "Commune Sanctorum" is followed by a series of "votive Masses," *e.g.*, the Mass of the Holy Ghost, the Mass of the Blessed Sacrament, &c., and these again by the Masses for the deceased. The same part of the Missal likewise contains a long series of collects for particular intentions, "ad libitum sacerdotis," many of which are of quite singular beauty.

Next follow, or may follow, certain authorized supplements, of which the first ("Pro aliquibus locis") forms part of the body of the Missal. This contains the Masses for a number of feasts which, though not universally observed, have been conceded to more than one country or region. The supplements for particular dioceses, or groups of dioceses *(e.g.*, those of England and Wales), and for particular religious orders, are published separately. And it may be useful to warn the reader that, in ordering a Missal from a publisher or bookseller, care should be taken to specify the supplements required, so that they may be bound up with the Missal. Some religious orders, however, have not merely a supplement, but a special Missal of their own, identical of course, in substance, with the "Missale Romanum," though differing from it in certain details.

It has already been mentioned that the nucleus of the Roman Missal, so far as its non-choral portions are concerned, is or was to be found in the copy of St. Gregory's Sacramentary sent by Pope Hadrian I to Charlemagne. About this book a few words must here be added. The transaction is recorded in a letter written by the Pope to the Emperor between the years 784 and 791. He says in effect: "You have asked us to send you an uninterpolated (*immixtum*) copy of the Sacramentary

Chapter IV: The Roman Missal and Its Ancestry

arranged by our holy predecessor Pope Gregory. This we now do by the hands of John, Abbot of Ravenna."[3] So much is clear, but it is unfortunately no less certain that not one of the many extant MS. copies of the "Gregorianum," as we may henceforth call it, is by any means "immixtum," for all of them have been, as Dom S. Baumer has pointed out, "largely augmented from other sources," mainly, perhaps, Gallican. It is true that, within a generation of the arrival of Hadrian's MS., a serious and presumably successful attempt was made, by an editor who is believed to have been Alcuin, to purge the already inflated Gregorianum of its alien elements. So far as he adopted the plan of relegating these to a kind of supplement, or second and third "book," separated from the older portion of the work by a "praefatiuncula" or "little preface" of his own (known as the "Hucusque"), his task of careful discrimination has been effective. But in many cases he was content to leave inserted material in the position in which he found it, merely indicating the later additions by means of asterisks or obeli. And it unfortunately happened that, notwithstanding his stringent directions, copyists omitted to reproduce these diacritical marks. Hence, to the question: "Can we restore St. Gregory's Mass-book?" the answer must needs be, if not wholly negative, at best a very hesitating affirmative.[4] The question, however, concerns only the antiquity of particular Masses, and other points of quite secondary importance. It in no way affects the substance or general structure of the book, the whole of which is, of course, included in the later and "largely augmented" copies.

But the Gregorianum was not the earliest Roman Mass-book to gain a wide circulation. Indeed, a careful examination of numerous ninth-century catalogues of cathedral and monastic libraries led Baumer to the conclusion, now I think

---

[3] Cod. Carol., ed Jaffe, p. 274; *apud* Duchesne, *Origines*, p. 114.

[4] See an excellent article by Mr. E. Bishop in the *Dublin Review*, October, 1894. From this article Baumer's words (above) are quoted.

generally accepted, that the purpose of Hadrian's gift was not—as used to be supposed—the substitution of the Roman for the early Gallican liturgy throughout the Frankish dominions, but rather the substitution of a correct and up-to-date Roman book for an earlier one, likewise Roman, which had for the most part already supplanted the old Gallican sacramentaries. This earlier Roman book is described in the catalogues as "Gelasian." In Rome the "Gelasianum," even in its original shape, had long since become obsolete, under stress of the liturgical reform introduced by St. Gregory. The nature of this reform is compendiously described by "John the Deacon," his biographer. "He reduced within the limits of a single book the Gelasian codex of Masses, eliminating much, effecting a few transpositions, and making some additions."[5] And this is all that we are told about the relation of the Gregorianum to the Gelasianum as regards the general structure of the two works. Of particular changes in detail, introduced by St. Gregory, mention will be made later, as occasion offers.

Of the Gelasianum several manuscript copies are extant, though, strange to say, not one of them mentions the name of its author or compiler in its title or superscription.[6] But there are, as it seems to me, no adequate grounds for calling in question the ascription of books of this type, at least as regards their chief contents, to Gelasius I (c.. 490). It is, however,

---

[5] "Sed et Gelasianum codicem de Missarum solemniis, multa subtrahens, pauca convertens, nonnulla vero superadjiciens ... in unius libri volumine coarctavit" *(Vita* ii. 17; *P.L.* lxx. viii. 94). Simple as this statement seems at first sight, it must be admitted that the words which follow "superadjiciens," viz. "pro exponendis evangelicis lectionibus" have puzzled and baffled all the commentators. Nor can I pretend to explain them. There is nothing in the Gregorianum which can be said to serve "for the exposition of the Gospel lessons."

[6] Bona (ii. v. 4) "suspects" that the Vatican Cod. *Reg.* 316 "contains the Ordo of Gelasius." This is the MS. which Tommasi, Muratori, Vezzosi, and in our own days Mr. H. A. Wilson, have edited as "The Gelasian Sacramentary." Mr. Wilson has of course collated other MSS.

Chapter IV: The Roman Missal and Its Ancestry

recognized on all hands that, even in the earliest of them all, the original text has almost certainly been somewhat thickly overlaid with extraneous matter, from which the task of separating out the original text can hardly be said to have been attempted with any near approach to completeness. Not only are there extensive interpolations from Gallican sources, but every known MS. of the Gelasianum has been to a greater or less extent "Gregorianized," particularly as regards the Canon of the Mass. Probst's observation that those sections in the Gelasianum which have the word "Ordo" in their title are of later date that those which have for their superscription "Orationes et preces," at least deserves mention.[7] For present purposes, however, it must be enough to say (**1**) that the Gelasianum, as represented by the earliest extant MS., is in three "books" (reduced by St. Gregory to one); and (**2**) that it has a very much larger number of collects (usually two for each Mass), of variable prefaces, and of variable clauses in the Canon of the Mass, than the Gregorianum.

Older still than the Gelasianum, but of quite a different character, is the so-called "Leonine Sacramentary" or Leonianum, which, however, has nothing to do with St. Leo the Great (c.. 450), except that it probably dates from shortly after his time, and that many of its prayers are adaptations of passages from his sermons.[8] Of the Leonianum only one copy, a Verona MS., is known to exist, or, perhaps, ever existed. The number of collects, prefaces, and even of complete Masses for one and the same day, is at first sight almost bewildering; and it is now commonly acknowledged that it never was an official Mass- book, but was rather in the nature of a private collection,

---

[7] Probst (herein following Tommasi) *Die altesten romischen Sakramentarien u. Ordines*, pp. 171 f.

[8] Havard, *Centonisations Patristiques dans les Formules Liturgiques* (Appendix II. to Cabrol, *Origines*, &c.), pp. 133 ff.

from which prayers might be taken more or less *ad libitum*.[9] Probst, however, suggests that this multiplicity of Masses for a single feast (*e.g.* that of St. Lawrence) is to be explained by the simple hypothesis that the compiler has faithfully recorded the various local usages followed respectively in the several churches dedicated to one and the same saint.[10] He also gives reasons based on internal evidence, for thinking that a considerable number of the prayers preserved in the Leonianum are to be ascribed to St. Damasus (c. 375), to whom with some probability, but without any positive evidence, he attributes the introduction of variable elements—collects, prefaces, &c.—into the Roman rite.[11] However this may be, there can be no doubt that many of the Leonine prayers are of great beauty and not a few of them have been preserved in the Roman Missal of today.[12] The MS. is unfortunately imperfect at the beginning and contains no text of the Canon.[13]

Beyond this point it is impossible to trace the ancestry of the Roman Missal in, so to say, the direct line. Indeed, from the aforesaid characteristic features of the *Leonianum*, the Ballerini draw the conclusion that at the time of its compilation no official Mass-book can have been in existence, and consequently that the *Gelasianum*, in its original form, must

---

[9] So Cabrol, *Origines*, p. 109; Fortescue, p. 118, note 5. But in fact the observation that the Leonianum is an unofficial compilation was made long ago by the brothers Ballerini in their preface to vol. ii. of the works of St. Leo (*P.L.* lv. 15 ff.), as was pointed out in *The Tablet*, 1896, ii. 1008.

[10] Probst, *Sakramentarien*, pp. 88 f.

[11] *Ibid.*, pp. 62 ff.

[12] For instance, the exquisitely perfect prayer (analyzed by Cabrol, pp. 110, 111) "Deus qui humanae substantiae," etc., used for the blessing of the water in the Offertory of the Mass.

[13] For fuller information on these three Mass-books, see the Introductions and notes in *P.L.* lv., lxxii., lxxviii., and in the standard editions of Feltoe (Leonine) and Wilson (Gelasian); Probst, *op. cit.;* Baumer, *Das so-genannte S. Gelasianum;* E. Bishop in *Dublin Review,* l.c.; Cabrol, l.c.; Lucas in *The Tablet*, 1896, ii. 1007 ff.; 1897, I. 86 ff., ii. 204 ff; and Fortescue, pp. 117 ff.

Chapter IV: The Roman Missal and Its Ancestry

have been the earliest of its kind.[14] Yet of what may be called collateral ancestors there are several, viz., the four or five extant early Gallican Mass-books, the conventional titles of which are given below.[15] In Chapter XVI. convincing reasons, as they seem to me, will be giving for holding that the ultimate origin of the Gallican rite was Roman, and that consequently the Gallican rite, by which I mean the form of liturgy which prevailed not only in Gaul and Spain, but in Northern Italy, and possibly also in remoter Ireland, from the fourth to the seventh century, may be expected to throw light on the very obscure history of the Roman Mass in its earlier stages of development. In the meanwhile this brief statement may be sufficient to justify such references as may be made, in the intervening chapters, to Gallican sources.

---

[14] *Praefatio*, &c., n. 12 (P.L. lv. 17 f.).

[15] They are (1) the Reichenau Mass-book edited by Mone in 1853, (2) the "Missale Gothicum," (3) the "Missale Francorum," and (4) the "Sacramentarium Gallicanum," now commonly known as "the Bobbio Missal." To these may be added, as illustrating the subject, the Ambrosian, and Mozarabic, and "Stowe" (Celtic) Missals; and also the description of the Gallican and Spanish liturgies, which are in substance one, by St. Germanus of Paris and St. Isidore of Seville respectively. More particular references will be given later.

CHAPTER V
THE LITURGY: HIGH MASS AND LOW MASS: SURVIVALS AND ACCRETIONS

ROM the foregoing considerations on the sources of the Roman liturgy, we pass now to the study of the prayers and ceremonies with which, in accordance with the prescriptions of the Church, the central act of sacrifice Roman rite, accompanied and surrounded; in other words, with the sacred liturgy as for centuries past it has been carried out, with a few local exceptions, throughout western Christendom. "For the most part," writes Mr. Edmund Bishop, "Catholics are content, where the sacred liturgy is concerned, to take in an even, not to say indifferent, spirit, the good that comes to them, without enquiring too particularly how it came. They are content in a general way with the fact that they are in the full current and stream of an uninterrupted tradition, the source of which is to be found in the apostolic age itself. Still, it should be even for Catholics a subject of interest to ascertain in some manner the steps by which the Mass-book in use today came to be what it is; and to trace the gradual accretions that have gathered round the primitive kernel.[1]

Now it might, perhaps, be expected that, in dealing with the prayers and ceremonies of the Mass as we know them, a writer should start with those parts of the liturgy which are more central, fundamental and primitive. But there may be some advantage, on the other hand, in clearing the ground by

---

[1] E. Bishop, "The Earliest Roman Mass-book," in *Dublin Review*, October, 1894.

first of all dealing with certain portions and features of the Mass which are of secondary importance, and of a less venerable antiquity than the prayers which more immediately accompany and surround the essential act of sacrifice. This is what I propose to do in the present chapter.

Many of us are so thoroughly accustomed to regard "Low Mass" as the ordinary form of celebration, and to think of "High Mass" as a more or less exceptional solemnity suitable for special occasions, that it may require something of an effort to bear in mind the unquestionable fact that High Mass is the normal type, of which, so far as the non-essential ceremonies are concerned, Low Mass is a kind of abridged edition. And the nature of the abridgment may be indicated by saying that, in Low Mass, besides the omission of the chant and the incense, the functions of deacon and sub-deacon are performed by the celebrant. As an illustration of this latter may be mentioned the circumstance that, while he reads the Epistle, the celebrant, who is then acting (so to say) as sub-deacon, holds the book, just as the sub-deacon does when he chants the Epistle at a High Mass; whereas when he reads the Gospel, the celebrant keeps his hands joined, as the deacon does while the book is held for him at the chanting of the Gospel. Moreover, as the deacon, when he sings the Gospel in a High Mass, faces the north (originally, perhaps, because it was thought right that he should face the bishop's throne), so in a Low Mass the Missal is placed, for the reading of the Gospel, slantwise upon the altar, and the celebrant stands facing as nearly northwards as the circumstances of his position conveniently permit. (The church is, of course, assumed to be correctly "orientated" with the great doors at the west end, and the altar towards the east. When this is not the case, the terms "north," "east," &c., are still retained for convenience of designation or description.) Another item in Low Mass which finds its explanation only in the fuller ceremonies of High Mass, is the position of the "Lavabo." Why should the celebrant wash his fingers just after

Chapter V: The Liturgy, High Mass and Low Mass   39

the offering of the unconsecrated host and chalice? That the act is symbolical of the perfect purity of heart with which he should approach the sacred mysteries is perfectly true; but why is it placed precisely here? For the simple reason that, in a High Mass, the offering of the bread and wine is immediately followed by the censing of the oblata and of the altar: and since this is a process which might easily cause some slight accidental soiling of the fingers, it is perfectly natural and congruous that, as soon as the celebrant has in his turn been censed by the deacon, he should find the acolytes ready with the water-cruet, the basin, and the towel. The censing being omitted in a Low Mass, the "Lavabo" has nevertheless been retained, mainly, no doubt, by reason of its symbolic significance. The need for a washing of the fingers would, of course, be more evident when "loaves and flasks of wine" were offered and received by the celebrant at this point of the service.[2] It may be of interest to note that, in the Ambrosian rite, the celebrant washes his fingers again immediately before the consecration, at the point where, in the Roman liturgy, he wipes them lightly on the corporal.

Of the preliminary portion of the Mass, which includes all that is said and done before the collect, it may be said that it consists of a number of more or less fragmentary survivals from the fuller ritual of a pontifical High Mass, or rather of the Mass as solemnly celebrated by the Pope himself in the sixth or seventh century. That our latter-day Roman Missals have been developed from an ancient Papal Mass-book is indicated, as has been said, by the titles or superscriptions "Statio ad S. Mariam Majorem," and the like, which stand at the head of the Masses for the Advent Sundays, for Christmas Day and the festivals which immediately follow it, for the Epiphany, Septuagesima, Sexagesima and Quinquagesima, and for each of the days of Lent, Easter Week (including Low Sunday), and Whitsun Week (not including Trinity Sunday), the Rogation days, the Ember

---

[2] Fortescue, p. 310.

days, Whitsun-eve, and (by reason of the litanies) St. Mark's day, April 25th. February 2nd, the feast of the Purification of our Lady, or Candlemas, was likewise a stational day, but the indication has dropped out of our modern Missals.

The blessing of the candles, it should be observed, is attached to the day of the month, whereas the feast is liable to be displaced and transferred, if it should fall on a Sunday.

In the first of the "Ordines Romani" published by Mabillon, we have a graphic description of the observance of the Roman "Stations." "The curious reader," says Fr. Thurston, "may there find narrated how the assembly of the clergy and officials meets first at some church used as a *rendezvous*, where the procession is formed to set out to the station of the day. The sacred ministers are grouped around the Pope in order of due precedence, according to their special functions. The acolytes go in front, walking, but the papal deacons with their *primicerius* ride on horseback, as does the Pope himself. Immediately before him, the Apostolic sub-deacon bears a processional Cross, while at his side the *stratores* help to clear the way and keep off the crowd. The clergy of the church where the station is held come out to meet the Pope, and conduct him to the sacristy, where he is vested for Mass with the same solemnity with which the vesting of a bishop now takes place at the beginning of a pontifical function.... Before the assembly is dismissed [at the end of Mass], a regionary subdeacon announces from the foot of the altar that on the next day that station will be held at such and such a church, to which the choir answer: 'Thanks be to God.' "[3]

---

[3] Thurston, *Lent, &c.*, pp. 155 ff. (abridged); P.L., lxxviii. 937 ff. With reference to the "Ordines Romani" it may be noted here that although, in Mabillon's edition and Migne's reprint, the first four among them are arranged in chronological order, the seventh, to which reference will be made hereafter, is of earlier date than any of them. It owes its position in the series to the fact that it deals with a particular set of ceremonies, viz., those connected with the "Scrutinies," not with the normal celebration of a pontifical Mass. *Cf.* Probst, *Sakramentarien*, pp. 398 ff.

Chapter V: The Liturgy, High Mass and Low Mass 41

The psalm "Judica me Deus," with its antiphon "Introibo ad altare Dei," though now said by the celebrant at the foot of the altar, was originally what may be described as his private "Introit"; that is to say it was the psalm which, first as a matter of laudable custom, and afterwards by rule and precept, he recited on his way from the sacristy to the altar, while the choir sang the "Introit" proper to the day. How entirely appropriate to the purpose specified is the psalm, and more particularly the antiphon, may be illustrated by a passage from the ancient tract "de Sacramentis," traditionally attributed to St. Ambrose, and perhaps compiled from his instructions. Addressing the neophytes who have just received baptism on Holy Saturday or Whitsun-eve, the writer says: "You came, then, full of desire, to the altar; you came ... to the altar that you might thence receive the Sacrament. Let your soul exclaim: 'I will go unto the altar of God, to God Who giveth joy to my youth.' You have laid aside the decrepitude of sin, you have taken on the grace of youth; this is the gift which the heavenly sacraments have bestowed on you. Hear David saying: 'Thy youth shall be renewed as the eagle's,' " etc.[4]

The passage only repeats, in a somewhat amplified form, what St. Ambrose himself had more briefly said in the eighth chapter of the tract "de Mysteriis."[5] As regards the date and provenance of the "de Sacramentis," internal evidence points to northern Italy, and to a time when Arianism was still rampant. No other heresy is alluded to, and the tract is therefore at least as old as the early part of the fifth century.[6] The suggestion that the tract may have been taken down by a stenographer from the instructions of St. Ambrose himself, and destined at first, by reason of the "disciplina arcani" then in full force, for private

---

[4] *De Sacram.* IV. ii. 7 (*P.L.* xvi. 437)

[5] *P.L.* ibid. 403.

[6] Cf. Duchesne, *Origines*, p. 169.

circulation, is Probst's.⁷

The passage, however, does not, as Bona points out, either prove or indicate that either antiphon or psalm were already, in the fifth century, recited by the celebrant on his way to the altar; and we must be content to know that the usage had become thoroughly established about the time of the Norman Conquest.⁸

The joyful access to the altar heralded by this psalm receives, however, in the case of one who is not fresh from the waters of baptism, a check at the thought of sin; and the psalm is appropriately followed by the "Confiteor." A child's hymn gives a simple expression to the leading thoughts of both.

> Now to God's altar will I go
> That He with joy may fill my youth:
> That sin's dark ways I may not know
> But walk by light of God's own truth.⁹
> But I am weak and wayward, Lord,
> And from the path too oft have strayed;
> The fault is mine; Thine the reward
> Of pardon for confession made.
> With grief sincere I now confess
> My sins of thought and word and deed;
> And that I may no more transgress
> Mary and all the saints will plead.

The "Confiteor," as we know it and use it, is the result of the "survival of the fittest" among many similar forms of prayer which were composed, though no particular form was prescribed, for the use of the celebrant and the sacred ministers while they either lay prostrate (as still happens on Good Friday), or knelt or stood at the foot of the altar, while the choir

---

[7] Probst, *Liturgie des Vierten Jahrhunderts*, p. 239.

[8] The earliest witnesses cited by Bona *(de Rebus Liturgicis,* II. ii. 3) are a MS. of perhaps the eleventh century, and the "Micrologus," an anonymous tract of approximately the same date.

[9] "Emitte lucem tuam et veritatem tuam," etc,

Chapter V: The Liturgy, High Mass and Low Mass 43

continued or concluded the singing of the "Introit."[10] I say knelt or stood, for although Father Thurston writes: "The Good Friday prostration probably represents an act of humiliation which was as habitually practised in the early Church, as the genuflection is with us, every time that the chief Pontiff and his attendants made their solemn entry into the sanctuary for High Mass," this seems to me to be too sweeping a statement.[11] Surely, for instance, there would be no prostration in paschal time. Nor do the words of the first "Ordo Romanus" suggest prostration as usual or habitual. "The fourth chorister precedes the pontiff, to place a cushion (or a faldstool, "oratorium") for him before the altar, and the pontiff on his arrival prays thereon (or thereat)."[12] This, however, is in the description of the Easter Mass. For the rest, it is but fitting that, before proceeding to the altar to plead for the people, the celebrant should first take his stand in the midst of those who represent the congregation, ranging himself for the moment with those on whose behalf he is about to offer the Holy Sacrifice.[13]

The "Introit," sung by the choir, and now, but not originally, recited by the celebrant at the altar, is said, in the "Liber Pontificalis," to have been introduced by Celestine I (c. 425).[14] It originally consisted of a complete psalm, to which the antiphon and doxology (*i.e.,* the "Gloria Patri") may have been added later. But the psalm is now represented only by a single verse, so that this choral piece now consists of an antiphon, one verse, usually the first of a psalm, the "Gloria Patri," and the repeated antiphon—a typical instance of a fragmentary

---

[10] Bona, *l.c.* n. 5.

[11] Thurston, *Lent, &c.,* p. 330.

[12] *P.L.* lxxviii. 942.

[13] On the contents and structure of the *Confiteor* see chapter xv.

[14] "Hic ... constituit ut cl. psalmi David ante sacrificium psallerentur antiphonatim (*i.e.,* not "with an antiphon," but by alternating choirs) quod ante non fiebat, nisi tantum recitabantur epistolae Pauli apostoli et sanctum evangelium, et sic missae fiebant" (*P.L.* cxxiii. 199 f.).

survival. It may be of interest to mention, in passing, an intermediate stage in the process of abbreviation. The psalm of the introit was, of course, sung while the Pope proceeded from the sacristy to the sanctuary. But it would often happen that he reached the sanctuary before the psalm was finished. And we learn from the "Ordo Romanus" already referred to, that when this was the case he gave a sign to the leader of the choir ("ad priorem scholae"), who thereupon sang the "Gloria Patri" without finishing the psalm.[15]

The "Kyrie Eleison," as we learn from St. Gregory himself, is the abbreviated substitute for a litany which still held its place, at least on certain occasions and in penitential seasons. What the occasions were on which the litany was said, St. Gregory does not tell us, but they were plainly not of rare occurrence, for he writes: "In quotidianis autem missis aliqua quae dici solent tacemus, [et] tantummodo Kyrie eleison et Christe eleison dicimus."[16] That the litany was characteristic of penitential seasons appears from the rubric in a MS. of the Gregorianum, which directs that when it has been sung the "Gloria in excelsis" and "Alleluia" are to be omitted.[17] It may be mentioned that the early Irish MS. known as the "Stowe Missal" begins, after a short antiphon, with what we now call the Litany of the Saints. But, seeing that one of the prayers which immediately follows has the colophon: "This prayer is sung at every Mass"[18] it may be inferred that the litany was not recited every day.[19] The litany which, in the Roman rite, was in

---

[15] *P.L.* lxxviii. 942.

[16] *Epist.* IX. xii.; *P.L.* lxxvii. 956.

[17] *P.L.* lxxviii. 25.

[18] MacCarthy, p. 195.

[19] It has repeatedly been observed (by Warren, MacCarthy, and others) that a fragmentary MS. of the Irish Abbey of St. Gall (one of St. Colombanus' continental foundations) begins, like the Stowe Missal, with the antiphon "Peccavimus," etc., which in the latter precedes the litany. But the very remarkable similarity even in strange details of the initial P in the two MSS.,

Chapter V: The Liturgy, High Mass and Low Mass   45

common but not daily use, though longer than the "Kyrie," would seem to have been notably shorter than what is popularly known as "the Litany of the Saints." The official title of this is "Litaniae Majores—the Greater Litanies," a term which manifestly presupposes the existence of "lesser litanies," now no longer in use. These may probably have resembled the series of petitions, each followed by "Domine miserere—Lord have mercy" which in the Ambrosian rite are still chanted or recited on the Sundays in Lent. There is moreover some reason for thinking that the lesser litanies were—in or before St. Gregory's time—transferred from the position which, as Probst believed, they formerly held after the Gospel. The greater litanies were, on the other hand, of a processional character. These latter still hold their place on Holy Saturday and on Whitsun-eve, on which days the final "Kyrie" of the litany serves as the "Kyrie" of the Mass.[20] The same may perhaps have been formerly the case on the Rogation days and on March 25th, on which days the "Litaniae majores" are also prescribed.[21]

The "Gloria in excelsis" is the Latin version of a Greek hymn which, in the Byzantine rite, forms part of the morning office ("Orthros," corresponding to our "Lauds"), but not of the Mass.[22] According to the "Liber Pontificalis" it was St. Telesphorus (c. 130) who first ordered that the "Gloria" should

---

has not, I believe, been noticed in any work on the subject; and I take the opportunity of calling attention to it here. The point of this observation is that from the close similarity of the MSS., so far as they admit of comparison, we should learn not to regard the Stowe Missal as an altogether isolated witness in liturgical matters.

[20] This is true, of course, only of the principal Mass on Whitsun Eve, when it follows the blessing of the font.

[21] Cf. Probst, *Abendldndische Messe*, pp. 123 ff., and (not quite in accord with him) Thurston, *Lent and Holy Week*, pp. 434 f.

[22] Brightman, *Eastern Liturgies*, p. 577 (s.v. "Gloria").

be sung at the midnight Mass of Christmas Day.²³ But this statement may probably have reference only to the opening words of the hymn, which is said, but on doubtful authority, to have been first translated in its entirety by St. Hilary of Poitiers (c. 350). Bona cites St. Athanasius for its use as a morning hymn, and observes that Alcuin (c. 800) is the first to mention the tradition concerning St. Hilary.²⁴ By Pope Symmachus (c. 500) if we may trust the "Liber Pontificalis," its use was extended to all Sundays and to the feasts of Martyrs.²⁵ With the exception, however, of Easter-day, it was to be sung only when the celebrant was a bishop; and this prohibition lasted during many centuries.²⁶ Berno of Reichenau, in his treatise "de Officio Missae" (c. 1030) argues at great length that there is no reason why priests as well as bishops should not recite this hymn at Mass.²⁷ And although Menard and Bona, commenting on the passage,²⁸ very pertinently remark that the quite explicit regulation on the subject ought to have been accounted a good and sufficient reason for abstention, we may well rejoice that the pious importunity of private devotion—tolerated as we

---

²³ "Hic constituit ut... natali Domini noctu missae celebrarentur (here we have the very origin of the midnight Mass)... et ante sacrificium hymnus diceretur angelicus, hoc est, *Gloria in excelsis Deo*" (*L.P.* in *P.L.* cxxvii. 1175 f). No indication is here given of the position of the "Gloria" in the Mass. This is doubtful by reason of the statement in the "L.P." that down to Celestine's time the liturgy began with the lessons.

²⁴ Bona, II. iv. He aptly justifies the use of the word "hymn" to describe the Gloria by quoting the words of St. Augustine (in Ps. cxlviii.): "Si laudas Deum et non cantas, non dicis hymnum. Si laudes quod non pertinet ad laudem Dei, non dicis hymnum. Hymnum ergo tria ista habet, et canticum, et laudem, et Dei."

²⁵ *P.L.* cxxviii. 453 f.

²⁶ So Menard's MS. of the Gregorianum: "Item dicitur, Gloria (&c.) ... si episcopus fuerit, tantummodo die dominico sive diebus festis. *A presbyteris autem minime dicitur, nisi solo in Pascha*" (*P.L.* lxxviii. 25).

²⁷ *P.L.* cxlii. 1058 f.

²⁸ Menard (note 9) in P.L. lxxviii. 268; Bona, *l.c.*

Chapter V: The Liturgy, High Mass and Low Mass

must suppose by a not too-exacting authority—should have at last carried the day, and that we are not only allowed, but commanded, to recite the "Gloria" in every festal Mass.

And here a remark and a digression may be allowed which may possibly help devotion. While it is a most excellent "method of hearing Mass" to follow the celebrant verbatim throughout the service with the help of the Missal, this particular "method" has at no time been prescribed to the laity. And even were it only by way of an occasional change, it may be useful sometimes to fix the attention on particular words or phrases and to dwell upon them for a while, developing and expanding them in our thoughts, after the fashion of St. Ignatius Loyola's "second method of prayer," without feeling bound to "hurry on" so as to keep pace with the priest at the altar. Among many words and phrases which thus lend themselves to expansive and affective reflection are those of the Gloria: "We praise Thee, we bless Thee, we glorify Thee, we give Thee thanks," &c., which do, indeed, strike the very keynote of the Eucharistic liturgy. Here is a simple expansion of these words in the form of a child's hymn or rhymed prayer (it makes no claim to be regarded as poetry).

An Act of Praise and Thanksgiving

All glory be to God on high!
We praise Thee, bless Thee, glorify
Thy name, and thank Thee, dearest Lord,
For all Thy gifts on us outpoured.
Ungrateful may we never be,
Forgetful of our debt to Thee.

We thank Thee for Thy lowly birth,
We thank Thee for Thy life on earth;
We thank Thee for Thy words and deeds,
So full of comfort for our needs.

We thank Thee for Thy passion too,

Wherewith our hard hearts Thou wouldst woo;
Thy sweat of blood, the scourging sore
That for our sins Thy body tore;
We thank Thee for Thy thorny crown.
And for the Cross that bore Thee down
Upon the road to Calvary,
And for Thy death upon that tree;
Lord, Thou didst bear it all for me.

And lest Thy love we should forget.
Another boon Thou addest yet.
Of all the best, Thy Flesh and Blood,
To be our soul's enduring food.
O wondrous gift! O love supreme,
Surpassing every thought or dream
Of man's dull heart! But Thou hast said:
"Take ye, and eat, in form of bread,
And drink the blood for sinners shed."

All glory be to God on high!
We praise Thee, bless Thee, glorify
Thy name, and thank Thee, dearest Lord,
For all Thy gifts on us outpoured.

Passing now from the preliminary to the concluding portion of the Mass as we know it, we shall find that the "Gloria" is not the only instance in which what was originally a kind of usurpation, prompted by private devotion, has come to have the force of law. As we all know, immediately after the postcommunion and the salutation, "Dominus vobiscum," with its response, the deacon sings: "Ite, missa est," i.e., "Go, you are dismissed," or, more literally, "Go, it is the dismissal." And yet, if we are well-conducted Christians, we don't go, but stay in our places. We wait for the blessing, and for the "last Gospel." These are plainly in the nature of supplementary accretions super- added to an earlier and simpler "use." And this fact accounts, likewise, for the apparently incongruous arrangement

Chapter V: The Liturgy, High Mass and Low Mass   49

by which "Ite, missa est" has an elaborate musical setting, whereas, unless the celebrant be a bishop, the blessing is not chanted at all. It will readily be understood that we have here the survival of a period during which none but a bishop was allowed to give the blessing at the end of Mass; and Dr. Fortescue is probably right when he finds the origin of the blessing, as given in non-pontifical functions, in that which bishops usually give as they pass the congregation on their way from the altar after any service.[29] But in fact the story of episcopal blessings at or towards the end of Mass is rather complicated; and both for brevity's sake and because it is of no living interest it may well be omitted here.[30]

In the Lenten Masses and on certain other occasions, as we all know, the dismissal is replaced by the words, "Benedicamus Domino," which may be construed as an invitation to stay for Vespers, as many of us, very laudably, do stay, when, on Maundy Thursday and Good Friday, Vespers are chorally recited immediately after the Mass. And the "Oratio super populum," which forms a distinctive feature of the ferial Masses in Lent is, I am inclined to think, closely connected with the combination of a late Mass with early Vespers during the penitential season. For the "Oratio super populum" is no other than the prayer proper to the Vespers of the day; and its introduction here may well have been by way of an abbreviated substitute for Vespers, for the benefit of those, and they would be many, who could not remain for that service. The reader will also remember the shortened Vespers of Holy Saturday, which

---

[29] Fortescue, p. 393. The Micrologus calls in question the existence, at any time, of such a prohibition as has been mentioned above. At any rate, he says in effect, if it was ever in force, it had already in his time been completely over-ridden by a custom so well established that any departure from it would be a scandal (*P.L. &c. 990* ff.).

[30] The confusion introduced into the subject by Menard (note 100, in *P.L.* lxxviii. 286 ff.) was long since cleared up by Bona, II. xvi., a point which deserves to be borne in mind by students of an otherwise excellent commentary on the *Gregorianum*.

are incorporated in the liturgy of the Mass for that day. Father Thurston's suggestion, to the effect that the "Oratio super populum" was specifically a prayer for those of the faithful who had not communicated, is, as it seems to me, of doubtful value, though it had been already made by the author of the Micrologus nearly nine hundred years ago, and is cited with approval by Bona.[31] Against it may be cited not only the "oratio super populum" proper to Ash Wednesday ("ut qui divino munere sunt refecti, caelestibus... nutriantur auxiliis") which quite plainly and unmistakably implies that those on whose behalf it is said have, in fact, received Holy Communion, but also several of the corresponding prayers in the Gelasianum. Thus on two successive pages of Wilson's edition may be found the following phrases, occurring in lenten prayers "super populum," viz. (1) "plebem ... quam divinis tribuis proficere sacramentis"; (2) "caeleste mimus quod frequentant"; (3) "plebs tua benedictionis sanctae munus accipiat"; and again a little later, (4) "populis qui sacra mysteria contigerunt."[32] It seems hardly possible to understand these expressions either of presence at Holy Mass or of the penitential ordinances proper to the season.

The "last Gospel," which normally consists of St. John's sublime prologue: "In the beginning was the Word," &c., owes its place in the liturgy to a devout practice of reciting this passage on the way from the altar to the sacristy. By a custom, long since legalized, but of relatively late introduction, when a festal Mass displaces that of a Sunday or "feria," the Gospel of the Sunday or ferial Mass is read as the last Gospel. This is at least the case in private Masses. In cathedrals and monastic or collegiate churches where the ritual can be fully carried out, two solemn Masses are celebrated, one of the Sunday or feria, and one of the feast.

---

[31] Thurston, *Lent, &c.*, p. 190; *P.L.* cli. 1014; Bona, *l.c.*

[32] Wilson, *The Gelasian Sacramentary*, pp. 19, 40.

Chapter V: The Liturgy, High Mass and Low Mass

It has already been implied that, etymologically speaking, the word "Mass" means, simply, "dismissal." The form "missa," for "missio," is analogous to other low-Latin words, having the same termination, which are to be found in liturgical documents. Such are "ingressa," the Mozarabic name of the introit, for "ingressio," "collecta" for "collectio" ("collectio" being the form used in the old Gallican Mass-books), "ascensa" for "ascensio," and so forth. The phrase "missarum (not "missae") solemnia" had reference originally, to the two-fold dismissal (1) of the catechumens, and in some cases of the penitents, either before or after the Gospel or the homily, and (2) of the faithful at the end of the service.[33] It may seem strange, but it is unquestionably true, that from these solemn acts of dismissal the liturgy of the Mass, as a whole, has taken its name. By a similar extension of meaning the term is used in the "Peregrinatio Silviae" to designate other services also.

---

[33] The point at which the catechumens were dismissed was not always everywhere the same, as will be seen later. See below, chapter viii.

CHAPTER VI
THE COLLECT, SECRETA AND POSTCOMMUNION

F the three main divisions of the Mass, doctrinal, sacrificial and sacramental respectively, of which something was said in an earlier chapter, each contains a variable prayer, or short series of such variable prayers, assigned to the particular day on which the Mass is celebrated, or, to speak more accurately, assigned to the Mass itself, which may happen to be a "votive" Mass.

The three variable prayers are, of course, the Collect, the Secreta and the Postcommunion. And although our immediate concern is with the first of these only, they have so much in common that they may be conveniently dealt with together.

The word "collect" ("collecta" = "collectio" = "synaxis") originally meant no more than "an assembly" or even "a crowd," as when the capitularies of Charlemagne decree penalties against those who, on certain occasions raise an armed mob ("si quis cum ... cum collecta et armis venerit").[1] And its earliest ecclesiastical use was similar to this, except that it signified, of course, an assembly or gathering for religious purposes. This meaning it continued to bear even down to the seventh century; for in several MSS. of the Gregorianum, under date, February 2nd (iv. nonas Feb.), we find the title "Oratio ad collectam ad S. Adrianum," and presently "Ad missam ad S. Mar. Majorem," which implies, of course, that the congregation assembled at St. Adrian's, and thence went in procession to St.

---

[1] Caroli Magni *Capit,* iii. 74, *apud* Bona, H. v. 9.
51

Mary Major, where the Mass was celebrated.[2] From the full form, "oratio ad collectam," to the shorter and simpler "collecta," the transition was easy and obvious, and thus we get the meaning "a prayer recited (or chanted) on the assembly of the congregation." It next lost this more special significance, and, in the Western Church came to signify any liturgical prayer of the same general type as those which served as "collects" in the more restricted sense. Thus, in the early Gallican Mass-books, the title "collectio" is given to a number of variable prayers occurring at various points of the Mass, *e.g.*, "collectio ad nomina," "collectio ad pacem," &c. In the Roman liturgy, however, the term "collect" is exclusively applied to those variable prayers which are chanted or recited before the Epistle, though these prayers often retain their name even when they are used on other occasions. Nor should a secondary and adventitious meaning of the term be overlooked. The mediaeval writers on the liturgy tell us that the "collect" is so called because, in it, the celebrant "gathers up" into a compendious expression the silent prayer and petitions of all who are present.[3]

On a majority of feast-days only one collect is said, but the number may be increased by one or more "commemorations," when these are prescribed by the rubrics, or by an "oratio imperata," i.e., a prayer added by order of the Bishop. Moreover, as a rule, ferial Masses (*i.e.*, Masses proper to particular weekdays) have at least three collects, exclusive of the "imperata." The next point to be noticed is that whatever the number of collects may be, that of the secretae and postcommunions is the same; or, in other words, that each collect has its corresponding secreta and postcommunion. Of the subsidiary collects which are said or sung when one or more lessons from Holy Scripture, in addition to the Epistle and Gospel, are read, something will be said in Chapter VII.

---

[2] *P.L.* lxxviii. 46.

[3] Bona, *l.c.;* Probst, *Abendl. Messe*, p. 126.

Chapter VI: The Collect, Secreta and Postcommunion

These variable prayers, proper to particular days or particular Masses, and all conforming to a certain structural type to be presently described, are characteristic of the Western liturgies, as distinct from the Eastern, which have nothing that corresponds to them in point of form and variability. And they undoubtedly deserve serious study. A "liberal" education is supposed to impart at least some appreciation of the beauties of classical Latin; but it is well to remember that ecclesiastical Latin has its beauties also, and that these are nowhere more apparent than in the collects, secretae, and postcommunions of the Roman Missal.

While these three classes of prayers have, as has been said above, certain general features in common, there are others which are severally characteristic of each class. To take the latter first, a very cursory examination of the Missal is sufficient to reveal the fact that whereas the collect is of more general import, the secreta almost invariably (and in the case of the older Masses quite invariably) contains a special reference to the Sacrifice ("haec munera," or "dona," or "sacrificia," "has hostias," or the like), while the postcommunion no less invariably has reference to the Sacrament, which, be it observed, all those who have been present at Mass are assumed to have received. By way of illustration it may be useful to cite the secreta and postcommunion of the Mass for the Wednesday in the third week of Lent.

S.—"Suscipe, quaesumus Domine, preces populi tui cum oblationibus hostiarum: et tua mysteria celebrantes ab omnibus nos defende periculis. Per Dominum," &c. ("Receive, we beseech Thee, O Lord, the prayers of Thy people, together with the sacrificial gifts which we offer," &c.)

P.C.—"Sanctificet nos. Domine, qua pasti sumus mensa caelestis: et a cunctis erroribus expiatos, promissionibus reddat acceptos. Per Dominum," &c. ("May the heavenly banquet wherewith we have been refreshed sanctify us, O Lord," &c.).

It is nothing short of a liturgical solecism when, in certain Masses compiled in comparatively modern times, the secreta contains no reference whatever to the sacrifice as such, but is concerned solely with the Communion. The re-awakened or reawakening liturgical sense of our own times will, it may be hoped, preserve the venerable Missale Romanum from any additional blots and blunders of this kind.

To return now to the general characteristics which are common to all these variable prayers, it will be profitable to consider carefully the structural type to which they all, more or less perfectly, conform. Every one of these prayers will be found to contain all or some of the following elements, and, for the most part, no others, viz.:

1. The invocation: "Deus," "Omnipotens sempiterne Deus," "Domine," or the like. ("O God," "Almighty and everlasting God," "O Lord," &c.)[4]

2. The "motive," very commonly, but not invariably, introduced by the relative "qui," ("who,"): e.g., "Deus, *qui corda fidelium Sancti Spiritus illustratione docuisti*" ("O God, *who hast taught the hearts of Thy faithful by the light of the Holy Spirit*"); or, "Deus, *cujus proprium est misereri semper et parcere*" ("O God, *whose property it is always to show mercy and to spare*"). Or again to take a couple of examples from Masses proper to Saints' days: "Deus *qui praesentem diem honorabilem nobis in beati Joannis nativitate fecisti*" ("O God, *who hast made this day honourable for us by the birth of blessed John*," i.e., the Baptist); "Deus *qui hodiernam diem apostolorum tuorum Petri et Pauli martyrio consecrasti*" ("O God, *who hast hallowed this day by the martyrdom of Thy Apostles Peter and Paul*"), &c. Sometimes the "motive" is expressed by means of an appellative or adjectival clause, or by a word or phrase "in apposition"; and in the

---

[4] Dr. Fortescue (pp. 249 ff.) gives an analysis of the typical collect which in some details differs from the above; but I see no reason for modifying what was already in print a year or more before the publication of his book (viz., in *The Xaverian*, 1909).

Chapter VI: The Collect, Secreta and Postcommunion 57

former case, as is obvious, "invocation" and "motive" are or may be in a manner fused into one. *e.g.*, (a) "Deus, *infirmitatis humanae singulare praesidium*" ("O God (who art) the support of human weakness"); (b) "Omnipotens sempiterne Deus, *salus aeterna credentium*" ("Almighty and everlasting God (who art) the everlasting salvation of them that believe"), &c. In a large number of instances, however, the "invocation" stands alone, without the addition of any specific "motive" for confidence.

3. The "petition." This is so obviously the very centre and substance of the prayer that it can never be lacking, and it hardly calls for illustration by examples, except indeed for the sake of completeness, and also for the sake of indicating the solemn simplicity and sobriety of language which marks these strictly liturgical prayers. Here are a few specimens:—

"Exaudi nos pro famulis tuis infirmis, pro quibus misericordiae tuae imploramus auxilium." ("Graciously hear our prayers for Thy servants who are sick, for whom we implore the aid of Thy mercy.")

"Da Ecclesiae tuae, eorum in omnibus sequi praeceptum, per quos religionis sumpsit exordium." ("Grant that Thy Church may in all things follow their precepts from whom it derived its first beginnings," *i.e.*, the Holy Apostles.)

(More briefly) "Fidelibus tuis perpetuam concede laetitiam." ("Grant to Thy faithful an unbroken gladness,") &c.

4. The "petition" is commonly, though by no means universally, enforced by the expression of a "purpose." It may be explained that, roughly speaking, the "motive" has special reference to God, being an appeal to Him in consideration of one or other of His attributes or acts, whereas the "purpose" has reference, more especially, to the needs of the petitioners, *e.g.*, to take first the instance last quoted, the "petition" and the "purpose" are thus expressed, the particle "ut" (—"in order that") introducing the latter:

"Fidelibus tuis perpetuam concede laetitiam; ut quos perpetuae mortis eripuisti casibus, gaudiis facias perfrui sempiternis." ("Grant to Thy faithful an unbroken gladness, *that* Thou mayest make them to enjoy eternal bliss whom Thou hast rescued from the perils of everlasting death.") Here, be it observed, much of the force of the Latin is lost by the unavoidable transposition of the clauses. This, however, is only one out of innumerable instances in which the terse elegance of the original refuses to lend itself to the exigencies of translation. Moral: All who can do so should by all means learn to use, and to love, the Missale Romanum, and not to be content with any poor, weak-kneed English substitute.

It should be added that, occasionally, the place of the "purpose" is taken by a secondary petition, and likewise that the petition itself sometimes takes, grammatically, the form of a "purpose," introduced by some such formula as "da, quaesumus, ut" ("grant, we beseech Thee, that"), &c. But on these departures from the normal type it is not necessary here to dwell.

5. Last of all, and apart from the body of the prayer, comes the "conclusion," of which the most usual form is "Per Dominum nostrum Jesum Christum qui tecum vivit et regnat, in unitate Spiritus Sancti, Deus, per omnia saecula saeculorum." Sometimes, however, the contents of the prayer require a somewhat different ending, *e.g., "Per eundem* Dominum," or, "Qui tecum vivit et regnat," where our Lord has been already mentioned, or again "... in unitate *ejusdem* Spiritus Sancti ... ," when mention has been made of the Holy Spirit, and so forth. The immense majority of collects and of secretae and postcommunions are addressed, as the student of the Missal will readily see, to God the Father. But, in accordance with our Lord's own precept, all such prayers are addressed to the Father "through Jesus Christ our Lord," and, in accordance with a venerable liturgical usage, the unity of the Three Divine Persons in the Blessed Trinity is always explicitly affirmed in prayers of this class. When, however, a series of collects is prescribed, the "conclusion" is attached only to the first and last

Chapter VI: The Collect, Secreta and Postcommunion

of them; and when a collect is used "extra-liturgically," *i.e.*, otherwise than in the Mass or the Divine Office, the "short conclusion" ("through Christ our Lord") is used.

Those who pay intelligent attention to the liturgical chant at High Mass, and in particular to the chant of the celebrant, will easily be able to discover for themselves that the intonations used in the singing of the collect and the postcommunion serve, as a rule, to mark off two at least of the main divisions indicated above. Two inflections, a greater and a lesser, occur in the body of the prayer, the greater for the most part coming at the close of the "motive," while the lesser concludes the "petition" and introduces the "purpose" of the prayer. When these prayers are correctly printed, as in the authentic "Missale Romanum," the place of the inflexions is indicated by a colon "punctum principale" and a semicolon "semi- punctum" respectively. These stops, it will be observed, indicate, not precisely "breaks in the sense" (as Haberl incorrectly says), but rather the logical divisions of the sentence, which is not quite the same thing. The following example may serve to illustrate this, the syllables on which the inflexions fall being indicated by italics and hyphens:

"Deus, qui omnipotentiam tuam parcendo maxime et miserando *ma-ni-fe-stas:* multiplica super nos misericordiam *tuam-,* ut," &c.

It will have been noticed that whereas the collect is usually introduced by the single word "Oremus," the series of collects which, on Good Friday, follow the Gospel, are each introduced by an introductory formula, in which we are invited to pray for the special intentions for which the several prayers are offered. That such invitatory formulas were in daily use in the Gallican liturgy will be shown hereafter, viz., in Chapter XVI. Whether this was ever the case in the Roman liturgy, except in the case of the "orationes solemnes" above referred to, is doubtful. Such formulae are indeed found in the ordinal of the Gelasian Sacramentary, but inasmuch as this book, in the form in which it has come down to us, shows unmistakable traces of Gallican influence, no certain argument as to the Roman use can be drawn from its testimony. Moreover, it would in any case be unsafe to argue from a very special ceremonial, like that of ordination, to a common use of such invitatories. Yet though the fact seems to have been overlooked by many writers, one such formula (fixed, not variable) is actually to be found in the Ordinary of the Mass, and is never omitted. I refer to the "Orate fratres," which daily serves to introduce the secreta. And since the secreta was and is thus prefaced, it is at least possible that the collect and the postcommunion may likewise have had, in the fourth century or earlier, their variable or fixed invitatories. It should also be noted that another somewhat analogous formula has survived in the words: "Praeceptis salutaribus moniti," which immediately precedes the "Pater noster."

Returning for a moment to the Good Friday collects, it will be remembered that, after the celebrant has chanted the invitatory, the deacon, with the words: "Flectamus genua," bids us all kneel down, after which, almost as though the deacon had made a mistake, the subdeacon sings "Levate," telling us to rise from our knees. The deacon, however, has made no mistake. What has happened is simply this, that whereas his summons to kneel down was originally followed by an interval of silent prayer, this interval—as a concession to human weakness—was gradually curtailed till the act of kneeling became, what it is now, a simple genuflection. "Flectamus genua," etc., is still said on the Wednesdays and Saturdays in the Ember weeks of Advent, Lent, and September, and in the morning office of Holy Saturday. There can, I think, be little doubt that the invitatory was originally sung by the deacon; and it is at least certain that it was the deacon who originally sang "Levate." Its transference to the sub-deacon may well have been occasioned by a desire to minimize the apparent incongruity to which attention is called above. Yet as a warning against hasty conclusions, it may be worth while to observe

Chapter VI: The Collect, Secreta and Postcommunion 61

that the liturgy of the Coptic Jacobites has a triple genuflection without any pause, the invitatory to "bend the knee" being thrice repeated.[5]

In conclusion, space may be found for a few specimens of complete collects, which may serve to illustrate not only the structural analysis that has been given above, but also some at least of the beauties of these altogether admirable prayers. The first three are taken from the "Proprium de tempore," and the last from the collection of "Orationes ad diversa" (prayers for special occasions) which may be found in the Missal immediately after the votive Masses and the Nuptial Mass, and which are too often overlooked altogether.

(*Eleventh Sunday after Pentecost.*) "Omnipotens sempiterne Deus (invocation), qui abundantia pietatis tuae et merita supplicum excedis et vota (motive): effunde super nos misericordiam tuam (petition); ut dimittas quae conscienta metuit, et adjicias quod oratio non praesumit" (purpose). ("Almighty and everlasting God, who out of the abundance of Thy loving-kindness dost surpass alike the deserts of Thy suppliants and their desires: pour out Thy mercy upon us; so that Thou mayest pardon what conscience gives us reason to fear, and mayest grant in addition what in our prayers we dare not to claim at Thy hands.")

(*Fourth Sunday after Easter.*) "Deus, qui fidelium mentes unius efficis voluntatis: da populis tuis id amare quod praecipis, id desiderare quod promittis; ut inter mundanas varietates ibi nostra fixa sint corda, ubi vera sunt gaudia." ("O God, who dost make Thy faithful to be of one mind and will: grant to Thy people to love what Thou commandest and to desire what Thou has promised; that our hearts may there be fixed, where true joy is found.")

(*Fifth Sunday after Easter.*) "Deus, a quo bona cuncta procedunt, largire supplicibus tuis: ut cogitemus, te inspirante, quae recta sunt, et te gubernante, eadem faciamus." ("O God,

---

[5] Brightman, *Eastern Liturgies*, p. 159.

from whom all good things proceed, grant to Thy suppliants that by Thy inspiration we may think of what is right, and that under Thy guidance we may do the same.") Could any petition be more simple and comprehensive or, in the original Latin, more forcibly expressed? It will be noted that here, by reason of the shortness of the prayer, the "punctum principale" is shifted forward to the usual place of the "semi-punctum," and the latter is omitted altogether.

(For the grace of humility.) "Deus, qui superbis resistis, et gratiam praestas humilibus: concede nobis verae humilitatis virtutem, cujus in se formam fidelibus Unigenitus tuus exhibuit; ut nunquam indignationem tuam provocemus elati, sed potius gratiae tuae capiamus dona subjecti." ("O God, who dost resist the proud, and givest grace to the humble: grant us the virtue of true humility, whereof Thine Only-begotten Son showed in Himself an example to Thy faithful; that we may never be so puffed up as to provoke Thine indignation, but that rather by submission to Thy will we may become the recipients of Thy gifts.")

In this chapter the position of the collect, as the first item in the Mass of the Catechumens, has been taken for granted. Sundry questions relative to its original position, and to the mutual relations of the variable prayers occurring in the several Western liturgies, may be more conveniently dealt with in subsequent chapters.

CHAPTER VII
THE LESSONS FROM HOLY SCRIPTURE

THE first of the three chief divisions of the Mass, apart from preliminaries and supplementary accretions, consists in the main, as has been said, in the chanting or reading of certain passages from Holy Scripture. To them, all else in this part of the liturgy is subsidiary. These lessons from Holy Scripture are nowadays commonly and popularly spoken of as "the Epistle and Gospel"; and the phrase represents, with sufficient accuracy, the more ordinary usage of our time.

Anyone, however, who is in the habit of using the Missal will have noticed that the first lesson, even when there are only two, is sometimes taken, not from the Epistles, but either from the Old Testament or from the Acts of the Apostles or from the Apocalypse. He may further have observed that on the Wednesdays in the four Ember-weeks, as well as in the fourth week of Lent and in Holy Week, three lessons are read, one from the Old Testament, one from the Apostolic writings, and (of course) one from the Gospels; that the Mass proper to the Ember Saturdays has six lessons (the number was originally twelve) besides the Gospel; and that on Holy Saturday, as part of the baptismal service, twelve lessons, called "prophecies," are read in addition to the Epistle and the Gospel, and six on Whitsun-eve. It is plain from the sermons of St. Augustine that in his day, and in Africa, sometimes only two lessons were read.

Thus: "Primam lectionem audivimus apostoli; 'Fidelis sermo,' etc.... deinde cantavimus psalmum ... post haec evangelica lectio decem leprosos ... ostendit." And again: "Prima lectio ... hodie ... est apostoli facta." Sometimes, however, there were three or more. Thus: "In omnibus lectionibus quas recitatas audivimus... primam ... Isaiae prophetae, quia omnia quae lecta sunt nec meminisse nec dicere possumus."[1] According to the "Liber Pontificalis," the practice of reading two lessons only, *i.e.*, the Epistle and the Gospel, was already well-established in Rome, in the earlier years of the fifth century. For, as has been seen above, Celestine I is there said to have introduced psalmody before the lessons, which, apart from special occasions, are distinctly said to have been two only. Yet there is reason to believe that at an earlier period the usual number, outside of Paschal time, was three. For the Gallican rite, derived originally from Rome, ordinarily had three lessons; the Mozarabic usually three; and the Ambrosian rite retains the three lessons on Sundays and all greater feasts.

Moreover, internal evidence seems to point in the same direction. The Bobbio Missal has three lessons on the first Sunday in Advent, on Christmas Day, on the first Sunday in Lent, in the "Missa in Symboli traditione," on Easter Sunday and in Paschal time (from Apocalypse, Acts, and Gospel of St. John), and in many instances under the heading: "Incipiunt lectiones cottidianis," (sic.).[2] Moreover it will be noticed that except in Paschal time, the Epistle is immediately followed, not only by the "gradual," but also by a second antiphon introduced and concluded by the word or phrase, "Alleluia," or, in Lent and on certain other occasions, by the "tract." Now when two lessons are read before the Gospel, the first is followed by the gradual, the second by the tract, or, in Whitsun-week, by the "Alleluia" antiphon; which at least suggests that the duplicated

---

[1] *P.L.* xxxviii. 950, 962, 262. Cf. Fortescue, p. 256.

[2] *P.L.* lxxii. 451 ff. So too St. Germanus: "Lectio prophetica suum tenet ordinem ... Quod enim propheta clamat futurum, apostolus docet factum. *Actus autem apostolorum vel Apocalypsis Joannis pro novitate gaudii paschalis leguntur.*" (Germanus, Epist. i. ibid. 90).

psalmody points to a "dropped" lesson.³ Unfortunately, however, for the peace of mind of "conjectural reconstructionists," the argument loses its force if we accept at its face value the statement of the "Liber Pontificalis," not only that Celestine introduced the singing of a psalm at the introit, but also that down to his time there was no psalmody at all "ante sacrificium"; which might be taken to imply that not the introit only, but also the gradual and Alleluia antiphon were added to the more primitive rite, after the lessons had already been reduced to two only; assuming that there once were three. But it is permissible to doubt whether the eighth century compiler of the "Liber Pontificalis" has rightly understood his authority, and whether he has not erred in ascribing to Celestine anything beyond the introduction of the "psalmus ad introitum"; or whether again, by "ante sacrificium," he really means anything more than "at the commencement of the liturgy."⁴

That the reading of the Gospel is surrounded with a more elaborate ceremonial than that of the Epistle is evident to anyone who has been present at High Mass. After the deacon has recited the "Munda cor meum—Cleanse my heart and my lips O Lord," and has received the blessing of the celebrant, a little procession is formed, consisting of the master of ceremonies and the thurifer with the incense, the acolytes with their candles, the subdeacon, and lastly the deacon who is to sing the Gospel. The announcement of the Gospel ("Lectio Sancti Evangelii," &c.) is greeted with the response, "Gloria tibi. Domine," and while this is being sung the book is censed. The "tone" of the Gospel is, too, more solemn than that of the Epistle, and at its conclusion, the book is carried by the

---

³ Duchesne was, I think, the first to call attention to this point. The compiler of the Stowe Missal designates the duplicated psalmody by the odd title "Psalmus bi-gradualis" (so in Probst's reprint, *Abendl. Messe*, p. 46, but not in MacCarthy, p. 199).

⁴ The passage has been quoted above, p. 54 (note 4).

subdeacon to the celebrant, who kisses the open page. Still more striking is the solemnity when, as in the Cathedral at Milan and in two or three of the more ancient churches in Rome, the Gospel is sung from an ambo or pulpit. All this special honour paid to the Gospel is manifestly in accordance with the fitness of things. But the Epistle also has its distinctive though minor solemnity. It is chanted by the subdeacon; whereas the other lessons, when there were more than two in all, were probably read, not by the subdeacon, but by "lectors," the very *raison d'être* of whose office was to perform this function. Dr. Fortescue, however, writes: "It was not originally the privilege of the subdeacon to read it," *i.e.*, the Epistle. "At first all lessons (including the Gospel) were read by lectors ... In the West as late as the fifth century the lessons were still chanted by readers. Gradually the subdeacon obtained the right to sing the Epistle as a consequence of the deacon's privilege of singing the Gospel." The number of sacred ministers had been reduced to two, so also had the usual number of lessons, "one minister sang the Gospel, it seemed natural that the other should sing the Epistle."[5] To this day the first lesson on Good Friday is read by a "lector," the second by the subdeacon; and the "prophecies" on Holy Saturday and Whitsun-eve are likewise read by clerics representing the "lectores" of earlier days.[6]

It may here be mentioned in passing that the gradual too was in pre-Gregorian days sung by the deacon. St. Gregory himself somewhere relates that this arrangement was apt to lead to an abuse, as deacons were apt to be chosen for their vocal powers. Accordingly the duty of singing the gradual was transferred to cantors, who, for the purpose, could not be allowed to mount higher than the steps of the ambo. Hence the name "gradual."

As regards the choice of the passages to be read in each

---

[5] Fortescue, p. 263, citing Reuter, *Das Subdiaconat*, pp. 177-185.

[6] Probst, *Abendl. Messe*, p. 108.

Mass, there can be little doubt that originally the Epistles and the Gospels were read continuously from the text of the New Testament, or rather of its parts, and that the words "Deo gratias" and "Laus tibi, Christe," which are now said by the server or assistants at the conclusion of the Epistle and Gospel respectively, are survivals of the sign originally given by the celebrant that the reading should cease. "The memoirs of the apostles or the writings of the prophets are read, as far as time permits," says St. Justin (c. 150).[7] And the giving of a sign to cease reading finds its parallel in the similar directions, occurring in the Roman ordines, that the celebrant is to signify that the singing of the psalm at the introit, or of the Kyrie, is to be brought to a close. In this connection it may be observed that down to the present day it happens on certain occasions that the reading in a community refectory is brought to an end by means of the ancient formula "Deo gratias," the use of which for such a purpose probably comes down by unbroken tradition from quite primitive times.

It is, however, almost certain that already in the fourth century the practice of reading the sacred text continuously had begun to give place to a system, or rather to sundry systems which varied locally, of fixed "pericopae," *i.e.*, to the assignment of particular passages to particular days or Masses. And it can hardly be doubted that the lectionary ("Liber Epistolarum et Evangeliorum"), in actual use is due to a partial fusion of several such systems. It is obvious that the Epistles and Gospels assigned to certain particular feasts and seasons, as for example, Christmas, Epiphany, Easter, Ascension Day, Pentecost, Advent, Lent, the Ember-days and Saints' days, have been chosen as specially appropriate to the occasion. But in the case of the Sundays after Pentecost, and of the third, fourth, fifth and sixth after Epiphany, *i.e.*, of rather more than half the Sundays of the year, it is impossible to discover any such

---

[7] Apol. I. lxvii. 3. "Lectio igitur erat continua neque fiebat per pericopas. (Rauschen, *ad loc.*)

special appropriateness. On the other hand, in the case of these very Sundays, traces are still visible, at least, as regards the Epistles, of the primitive method of continuous or successive readings. Thus the Epistles for the fourth, sixth, seventh and eighth Sundays after Pentecost are from Romans, for the ninth, tenth and eleventh from First Corinthians, for the twelfth from Second Corinthians, for the thirteenth, fourteenth and fifteenth from Galatians, for the sixteenth, seventeenth, nineteenth, twentieth and twenty-first from Ephesians, for the twenty-second and twenty-third from Philippians, and for the twenty-fourth from Colossians. The Epistle for the eighteenth Sunday is an exception, probably because the Mass of that day was originally intended to close the Ember-week. The sequence is resumed, so to say, on the fifth and sixth Sundays after Epiphany, on which days the Epistles are taken from Colossians and First Thessalonians respectively. This will seem the less strange if we bear in mind that, when the number of Sundays after Pentecost exceeds twenty-four, the Masses appointed for the last Sundays after Epiphany are used to make up the number. It is remarkable, too, that on each day, Thursdays excepted, from the Saturday before the fourth Sunday in Lent till the Saturday before Palm Sunday, as well as on all the Sundays between Easter and Pentecost, St. John's Gospel is read. And it is difficult to dissociate this fact from the circumstances that, on his own showing, many, if not all, of St. Augustine's 88 "tractates" on St. John were delivered during Lent, and those on St. John's first Epistle, in Paschal time.[8] Beissel, however, insists that no certain conclusion as to liturgical usage can be drawn from this; partly because it is incredible that the Bishop of Hippo can have delivered so many discourses within less than forty days, and partly because some of the "tractates" deal with only a verse or two of the

---

[8] Prol. in Ep. I Joan. (P.L. xxxv. 1977).

Chapter VII: The Lessons from Holy Scripture 69

Evangelist.[9] But St. Augustine's statement that, during the two weeks of the Passion and the Resurrection, he must needs interrupt his exposition, because the lessons appointed to be read during those weeks were so authoritatively fixed, is a clear testimony to the fact that a regular system of non-continuous pericopae was, if not yet established for the whole year, at least in process of establishment.[10]

For the rest, several of the Gospel lessons indicated by St. Augustine as assigned to particular days of the ecclesiastical year still hold in the Roman Missal the place which, in his day, they held in the liturgy of the African Church. And the schemes of pericopae drawn up respectively by St. Gelasius and St. Gregory—so far as they can be ascertained—show a gradual approximation to that which obtains at the present time.[11] It may further be remarked that, as in other points so also in the choice of the lessons from Holy Scripture, the Western Liturgies show a far closer relationship among themselves than with the Eastern rites.[12]

A word or two may now be said on the relation of the

---

[9] Beissel, *Enstehung der Perikopen des romischen Messbuches* (1907), p. 9. The tractates, he holds, rightly no doubt, were addressed, as "conferences," to a select audience.

[10] "Sed quia nunc interposita est solemnitas sanctorum dierum, quibus certas ex Evangelio lectiones oportet recitari, quae ita sunt annuae ut aliae esse non possint," &c. (St. Augustine, *l.c.*) Father Thurston *(Lent and Holy Week,* p. 167) has moreover compiled an interesting table of the Lenten liturgical psalmody showing unmistakable traces of an originally unbroken sequence. Cf. *Cath. Encyl.* i. 581 fif. An article by Dom G. Morin in the *Revue Benedictine* first, I believe, called attention to this matter. The facts seem hardly to square with Dom F. Cabrol's suggestion *(Origines Liturgiques,* p. 339) that the psalmody was chosen to suit the preceding lesson ("Il ne faut pas oublier que dans ces anciens offices la psalmodie et les legons sont en etroite connexion").

[11] Beissel, pp. v., 44.

[12] Beissel, p. vi. On the whole subject see also Fortescue, pp. 254 ff.

collect or collects to the lessons from Holy Scripture. It will be noticed, on reference to the Roman Missal, that whenever the Gospel is preceded by more than one lesson, the additional lessons, *i.e.*, those which come first, are separated, one from another, by a collect. And although, in a majority of cases, no special relation in point of meaning or purport can be traced between the lessons and the collects, yet, whenever such a relation can be traced, it is invariably between the collect and the lesson which precedes it, not with that which follows it. This is transparently clear in the case of the prayer "Deus qui tribus pueris," &c. ("O God Who for the three children didst temper the fiery flames"), which follows the lesson from the third chapter of Daniel on the Ember Saturdays. And a similar relation is not less plainly evident in the case of several of the Holy Saturday and Whitsun-eve "prophecies" and the prayers which severally follow them.[13]

Now these facts suggest a conjecture which may perhaps deserve consideration. Was not the Gospel, and perhaps also the Epistle, originally followed, likewise, by a collect? For such a sequel to the Epistle there is, it must be confessed, no trustworthy evidence available.[14] But in the case of the Gospel the question might almost seem superfluous, inasmuch as the word "Oremus," immediately following the Gospel (or, rather,

---

[13] Here one may cordially agree with Dom Cabrol when he writes (pp. 339, 340): "Les collectes ... surtout semblent la plupart du temps dependantes d'une priere litanique, d'une *lecture* ou d'une psaume qu'elles ont pour mission de completer ou de commenter" (italics mine). And (referring back to a previous note) it is probable enough that one of the causes which led to the break-up of the original continuity of the liturgical psalmody was precisely the desire to choose appropriate rather than merely successive psalms.

[14] The Stowe Missal has a collect after the Epistle (Probst, p. 46, MacCarthy, p. 198), or rather, it has two, one in the first hand, the other added (perhaps for alternative use) by Moel Caich; which at least shows the persistence of the usage in Ireland. But it is not safe to draw conclusions from the unsupported testimony of this somewhat wayward MS. The St. Gall fragment is not available for comparison here.

the Credo, which is however of relatively late introduction) to this day bears witness to the fact that something has here been omitted. For, as matters now stand, the invitation to pray is followed by no specific prayer, but by the "Offertorium," originally a psalm, which with its antiphon was not recited by the celebrant at all. Nevertheless, it is not quite clear what was the nature of the omitted prayer. Was it a single prayer of somewhat secondary importance, like the "Oratio super sindonem," which occurs precisely here in the Ambrosian rite? Or was it a series of intercessory petitions, identical perhaps, or all but identical, with those which follow the Gospel on Good Friday? Or is it possible that a twofold change has here taken place, viz., first the substitution of a single prayer, no other than the principal collect of the Mass, for the series of petitions aforesaid, and then the transference of this principal collect from its original place to its present position?

That this last hypothesis, with allowance for the inevitable crudeness of a too compendious statement, is the true one, several indications conspire, if I mistake not, to render at least highly probable. First of all, it is beyond doubt that the "preces solemnes," as we may conveniently call the Good Friday collects with their invitatories, were, in pre-Gregorian and pre-Gelasian days, chanted on many other occasions besides the one on which they have survived. For this we have the all but explicit testimony of Celestine I, and of the author of the fifth-century tract, "de Vocatione Gentium," who plainly allude to them as in common use.[15]

---

[15] "Obsecrationum quoque sacerdotalium sacramenta respiciamus quae ab apostolis tradita ... uniformiter celebrantur, ut legem credendi lex statuat supplicandi. Cum enim sanctarum plebium praesules mandata sibimet legatione fungantur,... postulant et precantur, ut infidelibus donetur fides, ut idolotrae ... liberentur erroribus, ut Judaeis ... lux veritatis appareat, ut haeretici... resipiscant, ut schismatici spiritum... caritatis accipiant, ut lapsis paenitentiae remedia conferantur, ut denique catechumenis... misericordiae aula reseretur" (Celest. Ep. xxi. 11, P.L. 1. 535; cf. *De Vocat. Gentium* i. 12, *apud* Probst, *Abendl. M.* p. 118, note 1).

On the whole I am strongly inclined to believe that a somewhat complex change has here taken place. If we may trust the analogy of the Eastern rites, this was the original position of the litany, that "lesser litany," originally a deacon's litany, of which something has been said in chapter VI, and which was followed by "the prayer—or prayers—of the faithful."[16] This latter prayer (or prayers), invariable in the East, gave place, in the Western rites, to the variable collect. And finally both the litany and the prayer or prayers which followed it were transferred—either simultaneously or successively—to the present position of the Kyrie and the collect. I suspect moreover that the litany, in its more or less primitive form, underwent a twofold development, viz., **(1)**, in its original position into the "orationes solemnes" now recited only on Good Friday, and (2), in its transferred position, into the longer processional litany known as the "litaniae majores," popularly called "the litany of the saints."

That, moreover, the collect was in fact transferred from its original place after the Gospel to its present position may be inferred with a high degree of probability from two independent considerations, viz., (1) that in the Gallican liturgy, whose Roman origin is here assumed, the place of the principal collect ("collectio sequitur") was undoubtedly not before the lessons but after the Gospel, and (2) the plain statement of the "Liber Pontificalis," that down to Celestine's time the service began with the reading of the lessons.[17] Nor is it difficult to divine a motive for the transference. For when, in course of time, the dismissal of the catechumens fell into disuse, and the

---

[16] Brightman, pp. 9 ff., 38 f£, 159 f., 223 ff, 264 ff. In the Byzantine rite the litany survives before "the prayer of the catechumens" but seems to have fallen out before the prayers of the faithful (ibid. pp. 275, &c.).

[17] The "preces pro populo" are placed after the Gospel by St. Germanus (*P.L.* lxxii. 92). And the "Sacramentarium Gallicanum" or Bobbio Missal invariably places the lessons before the collect, even in the "Missa cottidiana Romensis" with which the MS. begins. (*P.L.*, ibid. 451 ff.).

"Mass of the Catechumens" thereby ceased to have a distinct existence as such, there would no longer be any reason for postponing the principal collect to so late a point in the service; and its transference to the more prominent position which it now holds might well seem congruous and natural. To cut down superfluities was, as sundry indications show, one of the aims of Roman, *i.e.* Papal, liturgical reformers. It is however possible that the "transference" took place by two stages, viz. (1) by the addition of a collect before the lessons, and (2) by the omission of the collect after the Gospel, as now superfluous. In this case the Ambrosian rite, which has the principal collect before the lessons, but keeps a minor collect, the "Oratio super sindonem," after the Gospel, would bear witness to the intermediate stage; and would afford an interesting example of "arrested development." That a somewhat analogous change was made, at an early date, in the position of the Pax in the Roman liturgy, and that this change was probably due to similar reasons, will be seen in a later chapter.

In a later chapter, also, something further will be said about the gradual. As regards the Creed, it must suffice to say, here, (1) that it was introduced into the Eastern liturgies in the fourth century, as a protest against current heresies, but that its position varied in the various rites; (2) that it was introduced into the Gallican liturgy in 510; but (3) that the Roman Church, on the ground that it had never been affected with heresy, did not introduce it into the Mass till a much later date, possibly not till 1014, when the Emperor Henry in is said to have persuaded Benedict VIII to make the innovation. The date, however, though very positively affirmed by Berno of Reichenau, cannot be regarded as quite certain.[18]

---

[18] Bona, II. viii. 2; Fortescue, p. 288.

CHAPTER VIII
THE OFFERTORY

BY the "Offertory" of the Mass, in abroad and somewhat popular sense of the term—yet one that is recognized by Bona and other writers of repute—may here be understood all that is said and done between the conclusion of the Gospel, or Creed, or homily, as the case may be, and the commencement of the Preface. As a whole, the Offertory plainly pertains to the sacrificial portion of the Mass, of which it forms a kind of preparatory section, its nucleus or kernel being the preparation of the "oblata," *i.e.*, of the unconsecrated elements. In the Byzantine liturgy, and to a less extent in the other Eastern rites, this preparation has been developed into a somewhat elaborate service, the Prothesis or Proskomide, which not only precedes the liturgy proper, but, when the full ceremonial of a pontifical function is observed is (or was) carried out by a deputy or assistant priest at "the altar of the prothesis."

Dr. Fortescue apparently overlooks this quite characteristic feature of the prothesis, a feature doubtless often or even commonly omitted (just as many ceremonies of High Mass are omitted in a low Mass), and one which may even have passed into desuetude, but which was certainly once observed. "On this point the Byzantine liturgists are explicit and unanimous. From one to another, with merely verbal variations, they hand down the statement of the fact, accompanied with the traditional symbolic interpretation. The service of the prothesis, they say, symbolises the time of the ministry of St. John the Baptist, while our Lord was as yet hidden, and the deputy celebrant represents the Precursor whom the Messiah sent before His face to prepare His way."[1] When Dr. Fortescue writes that "in the East there is no Introit," and that "there is no procession of Entrance because the celebrant and his ministers are already in church when the service begins," his words most probably reflect, correctly enough, the current usage, but they certainly do not describe that of the palmy days of the Byzantine liturgy. There unquestionably is, or was, an introit, "eisodikon," sung at the "procession of entrance," sometimes called "the little entrance." And moreover, "the celebrant and his ministers" are, or were, not "already in church," but outside in the narthex; and what is more, all the congregation were there too, till the entrance of the bishop.[2] Brightman defines "The Little Entrance" as "the entrance of the bishop, after vesting in the narthex during the enarxis, with the people from the narthex into the church.[3] In the pontifical Mass, the bishop still first intervenes at this point, being fetched from the nave by the presbyters and deacons, a deacon carrying the Gospel." It is, however, a kind of misnomer, though of old standing, to call it "the entrance of the Gospel," inasmuch as on certain occasions the Gospel is not carried. It is the entrance of the bishop, preceded usually, but not always, by the Gospel. "In the absence of the bishop the procession ...is still made," from the altar by the north aisle and "back to the altar by the holy doors." The case is precisely analogous to that of a modern compared with an ancient procession. Originally as Father Thurston has somewhere said, a procession implied a place to proceed from, and another place to which the procession was made. In its modern and sadly shrunken form it is often no more than a circuit, starting from the altar and returning to the same spot. To sum up, "returning to the same spot," there is an introit in the Eastern liturgies, and the prothesis or anticipatory

---

[1] Lucas, in *Dublin Review*, April, 1893, p. 283, where full references are given.

[2] *Dublin Review*, l.c., pp. 289 fif. But see Fortescue, p.298, Brightman, p. 367.

[3] The "enarxis" is a short service which followed the prothesis.

Chapter VIII: The Offertory

offering of the elements is carried out before it by a priest of rank inferior to that of the pontificating bishop.

A very short preliminary service analogous to the prothesis and preceding the introit is prescribed in an interesting liturgical tract appended to the Stowe Missal.[4] And a somewhat similar usage is observed in the Mozarabic rite, and by the Dominicans at Low Mass. But there is, I believe, nothing at all to show that anything answering to the Byzantine prothesis ever had a place in the Roman rite, with which we are here chiefly concerned.[5]

The history of the offertory in the Roman Mass is somewhat complicated, and on many points so obscure that we are to some extent reduced to the necessity of employing the not very satisfactory method of probable conjecture. For present purposes the subject must needs be very briefly treated. One thing at any rate is certain, viz., that the offertory, as we know it, is the result of a twofold process, first of abbreviation and then of expansion. There can be no reasonable doubt that the interval between the Gospel (or homily or Creed) and the Preface was, at least on more solemn occasions, to a great extent occupied by two ceremonies which, so far as every-day practice is concerned, have completely disappeared from the Mass as we know it. One of these consisted in the successive dismissals of catechumens and penitents, with accompanying prayers; the other (already mentioned in the foregoing chapter) in the prayers for all orders of the Church and for "all sorts and conditions of men," heretics, schismatics, unbelievers, &c., whether in the form of a litany followed by a collect, or in that of the "orationes solemnes" which are still recited on Good

---

[4] MacCarthy, pp. 245 ff. (nos. 4-6). Another recension of the same, from the Lebar Breac, ibid. pp. 259 ff. (nos. 4, 6).

[5] "In all Eastern rites and in the Gallican ... a later practice grew up of preparing (and offering) the gifts before the liturgy begins. Rome alone kept the primitive custom ... of preparing them at this point, when they were about to be consecrated. The other practice is certainly later" (Fortescue, *l.c.*).

Friday.[6]

At how early a date the dismissal of catechumens and penitents passed into disuse it is impossible to say with any approach to accuracy, the more so because of the great variety of local custom. It seems clear, however, that whereas in the days of persecution such a dismissal at all Masses was a matter of necessity, in the course of the fourth century the ecclesiastical discipline as regards catechumens was more thoroughly systematised, the holy season of Lent (Quadragesima), and to a less extent, that of Paschal time (Quinquagesima, as it was often called) being set aside for their instruction. Hence, in the Gelasianum and in the seventh of the "Ordines Romani," which seems to be pre-Gregorian, we find elaborate and very interesting directions for the "Scrutinies" or examination of candidates for baptism, who are, moreover, throughout described as children. It is at least possible that the baptism of adult converts took place after private instructions, at Pentecost. The public "scrutinies" were held in successive weeks of Lent; special days being appointed for the successive ceremonies pertaining to them. But indeed the whole subject of the catechumenate is of sufficient interest to justify, by way of digression, a rather lengthy quotation from Father Thurston's admirable work on the ceremonies of Lent and Holy Week. It will be seen that his observations are in large measure concerned with the reminiscences of ancient usage which still survive in the rite of baptism, no longer carried out, as formerly, in close connection with the Mass. He writes:

> "For modern Catholics, to whom the word baptism recalls no other picture than that of a tiny infant beside the font in the arms of its godmother, it requires an effort of the imagination to conceive how much was done in the early Church to invest this

---

[6] See above, chapter vii.

Chapter VIII: The Offertory

rite of Christian initiation with every sort of solemnity.[7]

"Complete 'illumination,' to use a word which was technically employed in the Eastern Church as almost a synonym for baptism, was only imparted after two years' preparation and by slow degrees. At every stage the catechumen was wisely made to feel the unspeakable value of that which was being conferred on him in his admission into the Church of Christ. At every stage he was tested to see whether he were really worthy of the privileges of worship; and during the last three weeks of his catechumenate some little ceremony was gone through almost every other day, making an advance towards the climax of that wonderful Easter vigil when at last took place the triple immersion in the newly consecrated water, and the sacramental words were spoken which washed away all his sins and invested him with the spotless robe of sanctifying grace. ... There was in the first place a formal admission to the catechumenate, now principally represented in the baptismal ritual by the ceremonies which take place at the church door before the adult candidate is led into the baptistery. ... Then after the third Sunday in Lent, those who during the past two years or more had given satisfaction and had profited by the instructions given, were elevated to the dignity of 'electi' (chosen ones), or 'competentes' (fellow candidates), and during this last stage of their preparation they went through a ritual which appears in a condensed form in the second portion of our present baptismal service. ... We may note in particular the solemn delivery and recital of the Creed—in several parts of the world the 'Pater Noster,' a portion of the Gospel, and two of the psalms were formally imparted in the same way—and after that the renunciation of the devil."[8]

In the Gelasianum we find special insertions made in the Canon of the Mass on behalf of the candidates and their

---

[7] It is not, however, to be supposed that all the ceremonies described by Father Thurston formed part of a primitive liturgical usage. In their fullest development they are, I believe, to be ascribed to the fourth and fifth centuries.

[8] Thurston, *Lent and Holy Week*, pp. 170 ff.

godparents, similar to those which are still made, on behalf of the newly baptised, in the Masses of Holy Saturday and Whitsun-eve as well as throughout Easter week and Whitsun week. A reminiscence of the ancient practice may also be found in the lessons read on the Wednesday of the fourth week of Lent, which all have reference either to cleansing or to "illumination" or both.

The first is from Ezechiel, and contains the words: "I will pour upon you clean water, and ye shall be cleansed from all your filthiness"; and in the second, from Isaiah, we read: "If your sins be as scarlet they shall be made white as snow: and if they be red as crimson they shall be white as wool."[9] The Gospel recounts the healing of the man who had been blind from his birth, and was bidden to wash in the pool of Siloe or Siloam.[10]

It seems almost incredible that the candidates should not have been allowed to remain in the church for the reading of the Gospel, and for the homily which doubtless followed it. Yet the rubrics of the seventh "Ordo Romanus" clearly prescribe the dismissal of the catechumens before the Gospel. This, however, I suspect to have been the result of an innovation on the earlier practice, and one which did not permanently hold its ground. Its origin admits of a ready explanation. If the Creed and the "Pater Noster" were to be solemnly delivered to the candidate, why not the Gospel also? We have already seen, in the passage quoted above, that a "delivery of the Gospels" did, at least locally and at some period, form part of the ritual of the catechumenate. It is, in fact, elaborately provided for, under the title of "aperitio aurium—the opening of the ears," both in the Gelasianum and in the seventh Ordo. It took place on the Wednesday in what we now call Passion Week, when, in

---

[9] Ezech. xxxvi. 25; Isai. i. 18.

[10] St.John, ix. 1-38. This, however, is not the Gospel assigned to the day in question in the seventh "Ordo Romanus" nor is the lesson from Isaiah there found. (P.L. lxxviii. 996).

presence of the candidate, the initial sections of St. Matthew, St. Mark, St. Luke and St. John, respectively, were read by four deacons from four separate books previously laid on the altar.[11] That the practice, however picturesque and in some respects appropriate, was regarded as an innovation, may fairly, I think, be inferred from the fact that it was disapproved and condemned by more than one provincial or local council.[12]

The mention of these details might well seem irrelevant to the subject of the present chapter, were it not that a quite overwhelming mass of at least circumstantial evidence goes to show that, originally, the dismissal of the catechumens took place after the Gospel, *i.e.*, at that point in the liturgy with which we are here concerned. As regards the final "passing" of the custom, Bona observes that no trace of it is to be found in documents of later date than a.d. 700, nor is it mentioned, even by way of reminiscence, in the numerous mediaeval tracts or treatises in the Mass. To put the lowest limit at 700 or thereabouts seems, however, to savour of excessive caution, and Dr. Fortescue is probably right in saying that the dismissals had become obsolete a century earlier, viz., in the time of St. Gregory the Great, unless, indeed, it was he who gave its quietus to this ritual. No provision is made for "scrutinies" in the Gregorianum; and the survival of the warning "si quis catechumenus, recedat" ("if there be any catechumen here, let him retire") in the Holy Saturday ritual prescribed in the post-Gregorian "Ordo Romanus I", was probably no more than a mere formality.

I do not know on what grounds Dr. Fortescue dates the disappearance of the "orationes solemnes" or "prayers of the faithful" at about the same time. "They seem," he says, "to have shared the fate of the prayers for catechumens when the

---

[11] *P.L.* lxxiv. 1087 f.; lxxviii. 997; Wilson, *The Gelasian Sacramentary*, pp. 50 ff.

[12] Cf. Probst, *Abendl. Messe*, p. 121.

discipline of the catechumenate came to an end."[13] Is not this rather in the nature of a convenient rather than a well-grounded conjecture? There is no trace of these prayers in the Gelasianum except on Good Friday, and although one or two MSS. of the Gregorianum prescribe their use on the Wednesday in Holy Week, they form no part of the Mass for that day. On the contrary, it is clearly prescribed that they are to be recited some hours before Mass.[14] The argument from silence against the common use of these prayers in the time of St. Gelasius would seem to be of precisely the same kind as that from the silence of the Gregorianum with reference to the dismissals. As, however, they seem to have been in use in the time of St. Celestine, we are shut down to a period of about seventy years (430-500) as that during which they fell into desuetude. Their disappearance, it may be observed, is more easily accounted for if it be borne in mind that, as has been pointed out in chapter i., there is no evidence to show that they ever had a place in all Masses without exception, and that in all probability it was only on more solemn occasions, and more especially in penitential seasons, that they took the place of the "lesser litany" with its collect. Or if, with Probst, Duchesne, Fortescue and others, we adopt the hypothesis that their use was more frequent than I am disposed to believe, then we may also accept the further hypothesis, put forward by the first-named writer, that, as the ecclesiastical calendar of feast-days was gradually developed, and as in the Western Church it more and more powerfully affected the liturgy, the lengthy "orationes" were, by degrees, more and more frequently displaced in favor of the festal or dominical collect.[15] How and why the collect came to

---

[13] P. 294.

[14] *P.L.* lxxxviii 80 f. Cf. Ebner, *Quellen, usw.*, p. 213.

[15] Probst, *Abendl. Messe*, p. 119. His contention that the "orationes" continued to be said in the "Missa cottidiana romensis" has no support from the Gallican books, which (strange to say) alone, with the Stowe Missal, give this Mass. The "Deprecatio S. Martini " which the Stowe Missal places

Chapter VIII: The Offertory

be transferred to its present position is a question that has been dealt with in the foregoing chapter.

And now the question remains whether, in the Roman rite, the "nomina offerentium," *i.e.*, the announcement of the names of those who had made offerings for the Holy Sacrifice, or of benefactors in general, were, in the fourth century, read during this portion of the Mass. That such was the case in the early Gallican rite is I think beyond reasonable doubt. For the title "collectio post nomina" occurring passim in the Gallican books, together with the contents of many of the prayers themselves, sufficiently indicate that not only distinguished personages but particular individuals were named. Now the Gallican usage is most easily explained on the supposition that it was derived, ultimately, from Rome. And moreover, although the "orationes solemnes," and the litany which, as is here assumed, often took their place, were in themselves distinct from the reading of the diptychs or "recital of the names" in question, the latter would very naturally and appropriately be attached to them. Thirdly, certain abuses in connection with the reading of the names against which St. Jerome inveighs in a passage to be quoted later, can be more easily accounted for if the names were read at the offertory, than if they had, in his day, found a place in the Canon of the Mass.[16] And fourthly, an apt occasion for the transfer of the diptychs to the Canon might well have been afforded by the disuse, except on special occasions, of the "orationes solemnes," and by the transfer of the litany, to which (ex hypothesi) they had been attached.[17] The subject will be

---

between the Epistle and the Gospel would seem to be a specimen of the "lesser litany."

[16] See vol. ii.

[17] A fifth reason might be found in the prayer "Suscipe S. Trinitas" (the last before the secreta), which is, in fact, a slightly modified Gallican prayer "post nomina" (Cabrol, Diet, de l'Arch. Chr. i. 606), were it not that this prayer, instead of being a genuine survival from an earlier form of the Roman rite, seems to be rather in the nature of a later insertion from a

again dealt with in the chapters on the Canon.

Another rite which unquestionably had its original place towards the close of the Offertory, still using the term in its broad sense, was the giving of the kiss of peace. This is its position in all the liturgies, Eastern and Western, with the sole exception of the Roman; and it is all but impossible to doubt that this single exception is due to a transfer of the Pax from the position which it once held in the Roman liturgy likewise. This question will likewise be dealt with in a subsequent chapter.

But besides the dismissals, the "orationes" or litany, and the Pax, the offertory, as its name denotes, had for its central and essential element the bringing up of gifts or offerings for the Holy Sacrifice. Not, primarily at least, the offering of the gifts to God by the celebrant, but their presentation to the celebrant by the faithful. The gifts thus offered would seem to have been, in the first instance, bread and wine alone; then the custom crept in of offering other things as well, whether for the service of the church or for the support of the clergy or for the poor. Hence the necessity of regulations to the effect that nothing was to be offered, during Holy Mass, except bread and wine. Offerings of oil on Maundy Thursday, and of the first-fruits of the harvest and the vintage, either on certain specified days or when the season made them possible, were, however, permitted by various local regulations; and finally the making of a "collection," in the form with which we are all familiar, took the place of the older offerings in kind.[18]

The mediaeval rite, as carried out in Rome, may be thus briefly described. After the Creed, the pontiff or the celebrating bishop, attended by the sacred ministers, descended to the "senatorium," or—as we might say—to the altar-rail, to receive

---

Gallican source. Any references to the above-named work (not now accessible) are taken from notes on a single article, on the liturgy of the African Church, made some years ago.

[18] Bona, II. viii. 4 ff.

Chapter VIII: The Offertory 85

the offerings of the faithful, who presented their loaves "in fanonibus," *i.e.*, wrapped in linen cloths. Strictly speaking, the Pope received only the offerings of the nobility ("principum"). Those of the rest of the faithful were received by the bishop who was on weekly duty ("episcopus hebdomadarius"). The loaves were placed on a large extended linen cloth held by two acolytes. The wine was offered in flasks ("amulae"), from which it was poured by the archdeacon into a large chalice carried by the sub-deacon. This, in its turn, when it became full, was emptied into a larger two-handled vessel carried by acolytes. Meanwhile the "schola" or choir sang the "Offertorium." This originally consisted, like the introit, of a complete psalm with its antiphons ("cum versibus"), or of such a portion of the psalm as was sufficient to occupy the time consumed in receiving the offerings. These were then brought to the altar, the celebrant washed his hands, the deacon selected what was needed for the sacrifice about to be offered, and, after the "Orate, Fratres," the secreta was recited while the choir finished the offertorium.[19] Of this lengthy ceremonial, which was in use on solemn occasions more than a thousand years ago, a curious survival may probably have been witnessed by some of my readers at Milan. Here offerings of bread and wine are brought to the sanctuary gates by ten old men ("vecchioni"), and the wine and water by ten aged women, on behalf of the congregation, and are there received by the deacon.[20] It may be added that, in Rome itself, and wherever the Roman rite is observed, there is a somewhat similar ceremonial presentation of bread, wine and water, on occasion of the consecration of a bishop; while, on

---

[19] *Ordines Romani*, i. 13 f., ii. 9 f., iii. 12 ff. (P.L. lxxviii. 948 f., 972 f., 980 f.). For further details and interesting observations cf. Bona, II. ix. 1; Fortescue, p. 299.

[20] "Wickham Legg *(EcclesiologicalEssays*, p. 53) says that these offerings are not now used at the Mass actually in course of celebration, but at some later one" (Jenner, in Cath. Encycl. i. 401 B). Dr. Fortescue presumably has good authority for saying that the custom described above is "a foreign interpolation" in the Ambrosian rite (p. 300).

the still more solemn occasion when a saint is to be canonized, a procession of clerics enters the sanctuary, bearing not these elements alone, but candles and other symbolical gifts.[21]

It is to be noticed that no other prayer, except the secreta, is prescribed for this portion of the service, either in the Gregorianum or in the Roman Ordines. And, indeed, it seems clear that no other prayers were in fact recited, except perhaps as a matter of private devotion, during the performance of what Anglican writers term "the manual acts" connected with the reception and immediate preparation of the oblata.

To such practices of private devotion, to the operation of the principle of "the survival of the fittest," and to those Gallican influences which in more than one particular so powerfully affected the Roman rite, must be ascribed the gradual establishment of the existing series of offertory prayers, first as a matter of custom and then as part of the prescribed "Ordo," or, as we call it, the "Ordinary" of the Mass. These prayers are six in number, exclusively of the psalm "Lavabo,"[22] and of the blessing of the incense and the invocations used during the act of censing the oblata and the altar. They are (1) "Suscipe sancte Pater," &c., at the offering of the unconsecrated host; (2) "Deus qui humanae substantiae," &c., at the blessing of the water; (3) "Offerimus," &c., at the offering of the chalice, where the plural number indicates—what is sometimes forgotten—that the prayer should be said by the deacon together with the celebrant; (4) "In spiritu humilitatis," &c.; (5) "Veni Sanctificator," &c.; and (6) "Suscipe sancta Trinitas," &c.

---

[21] Among these gifts are a pair of doves in a cage, and another cage containing song-birds which in due course are liberated, and which symbolize, as they do in the frescoes of the Catacombs, the happy spirits of the Blessed. The present writer had the honour to take part in this function on occasion of the canonization of SS. Peter Claver, John Berchmans, Alphonsus Rodriguez, S.J., and of the Seven Founders of the Servite Order. Leo XIII on that occasion, I believe, ordered that the little birds should not be liberated within the building, as there they would starve.

[22] Ps. 25 (26).

Chapter VIII: The Offertory

Now it only needs a little attention to see that not only is the general purport of these prayers identical with that of certain portions of the Canon, but that they anticipate some of its very expressions. This is more particularly the case with the prayer "Suscipe sancta Trinitas," with its commemoration of the passion, resurrection and ascension, and of the saints. And this fact alone should be sufficient to make us suspect the unofficial and even the non-Roman origin of these items. For such mere repetitions are not in accordance with what has been described as the "austere simplicity" and the strict phraseological economy which is characteristic of thoroughly Roman compositions; and it is not surprising to find that most of these prayers can be traced back to Gallican sources.[23] As illustrating what has been said about "the survival of the fittest," these words of Bona may be worth quoting. "The prayers which are said at the offertory vary [or varied] in various churches, since, as the Roman Church for a long while did not employ them," *i.e.*, had no prescribed prayers for this part of the service, "each church adopted its own."

The prayer "Deus qui humanae substantiae" is, as Cabrol has observed, a Roman collect borrowed for its present purpose.[24] The statement, however, that the offertory prayers are mainly of Gallican origin, must not be taken to mean that in their sequence and purport they represent corresponding portions of the Gallican liturgy, but only that, taken singly, they originated for the most part "north of the Alps."[25] At any rate, whatever their provenance, there can be no question as to their beauty, and no one will now grudge the repetitions which, in combination with the Roman Canon, they involve. Dr. Fortescue has well said of these and other liturgical accretions to an earlier and structurally simpler rite: "If one may venture

---

[23] For details see Fortescue, pp. 305 ff.

[24] Bona, II. ix. 2; Cabrol, Origines, p. 110 f.

[25] Fortescue, p. 183.

a criticism of these additions from an aesthetic point of view, it is that they are exceedingly happy... The Eastern and Gallican rites are too florid for our taste and too long. The few non-Roman elements in our Mass take nothing from its dignity, and yet give it enough variety and reticent devotion to make it most beautiful."[26] If, moreover, it be allowable to suggest a thought which carries us a step beyond what is actually expressed in these prayers, we may suitably ask, at this point of the Mass, that as the bread and wine are to be changed into the Body and Blood of Christ, our hearts, too, may be changed into the likeness of His. And in this connection we may well invoke the intercession of our Lady. As the child's hymn has it:

> Now, at Thy altar, bread and wine,
> Thy priest doth offer; Thou, O Lord
> Wilt change them, by Thy power divine
> To Flesh and Blood, at Thine own word.
>
> At Mary's prayer, dear Jesus,
> Thou Didst change the water into wine;
> O take my heart, and change it now
> That it may be more like to Thine.

---

[26] P. 184.

HOLY MASS
VOL. II.

THE EUCHARISTIC SACRIFICE
AND
THE ROMAN LITURGY

PREFATORY NOTE

CONSIDERABLE portion of the contents of the present volume, notably Chapters X—XIII and XVI, will be found to be of a more contentious nature than those of its predecessor. But for this very reason it is only right to say that it would be a matter for very serious regret if, because I have found myself unable to agree with Dr. Fortescue on certain points connected with the history and structure of the Roman Canon, I should have seemed to underrate his really admirable and all but exhaustive study of the Roman liturgy. So far from wishing to create any such impression, the best advice I could give to any student who wishes to know more about the Mass than he can learn from these pages, would be to procure and to study Dr. Fortescue's more learned work. At its close he will find a very full bibliography of the subject; a fact which renders it quite needless to burden this little volume with a bibliographical appendix, which no one would be likely to use who lacks the opportunity of consulting Dr. Fortescue's treatise. To the reader who is familiar with Latin I would further recommend the study of Cardinal Bona's classical work, *De Rebus Liturgicis*. Dr. Gihr's treatise on the Mass, now happily translated into English, needs no commendation from the present writer.

Having in mind the judicious remarks of a friendly critic who has been at the pains of reading the proofs of the present volume, I take the opportunity of saying that, whereas my aim throughout has been to make the book sufficiently interesting to be popular, and at the same time scholarly enough to be helpful to the student, I have reason to fear that some parts of it (notably chap. xvi.) are of too technical a nature to engage the attention of the "general reader." To the general reader, I would venture respectfully to suggest that he may find it profitable to use freely the method of "skipping" such passages as may not appeal to him, rather than the easier one of tossing the book aside.

H. F.
St. Francis Xavier's, Liverpool, March, 1914.

CHAPTER IX
THE PREFACE

THE "Preface" of the Mass, as we know it, serves as an immediate introduction to the Canon, from which it is separated by the "Sanctus" or "Tersanctus." It is further distinguished from the Canon by being, within certain limits, variable, whereas the Canon, as its name denotes, remains, with the exception of a few special clauses, unchanged throughout the year. Hence to say that the Preface ought to be regarded as part of the Canon would be, so far as mere etymology is concerned, a sort of contradiction in terms. Yet that is precisely what, in view of the history of the liturgy and the true significance of its parts, one would like to say; and it is what, in effect, some early Latin Mass-books actually do say. In the earliest extant MS. of the Gelasianum the rubric: "Incipit Canon actionis" precedes the Preface; and the same is true of at least three other MSS.[1] At any rate, no mistake will be made if the truth be emphasized that the preface, with its preliminary dialogue ("Sursum corda," &c.) is an integral part of what in the Greek liturgies is called the "Anaphora," or, to use a thoroughly Roman term, an integral part of the sacrificial "Action."

For there can, I believe, be little doubt that, in quite primitive times, the great Eucharistic prayer, or prayer of thanksgiving, proceeded without interruption from the beginning of what is now the preface down to the end of what corresponds to our Canon, embodying in its midst, of course,

---

[1] Ebner, *Quellen u. Forschungen z. Gesch. des Missale Romanum*, p. 295; cf. Fortescue, p. 315.

the sacred words of consecration. The truth of this statement, at least in its general bearing, may be illustrated first of all by quoting, with some abridgment for the avoidance of repetition, the earliest extant description of the Mass.[2] This is to be found in the "Apology" (or "First Apology") of St. Justin the Martyr, who suffered death in A.D. 167. The "Apology" was addressed to the Roman Emperor, Antoninus Pius, about a.d. 150, the purpose of the passage in question being to refute malicious calumnies by giving a true account of what Christians were accustomed to do at their religious assemblies. Here then is, in substance, what he says:— "On the day called of the Sun, we all come together from town and country, and at our meeting the memoirs of the apostles, or the writings of the prophets, are read as far as time allows. When the reader has finished, the president (i.e., the celebrant) gives an instruction and an exhortation (νουθεσίαν καὶ πρόκλησιν)on what has been read.

Then we all rise and put up prayers (εὐχὰς πέμπομεν)[3] in common, both for ourselves and for all others wheresoever they may be, very earnestly (ἐκτενῶς),[4] to the intent that having attained to the knowledge of the truth the further grace may be vouchsafed to us that we may be found to be of good conversation by our deeds (δι ἔργων ἀγαθοὶ πολιτευταί), and observers of the commandments, whereby we may gain eternal salvation. When we have finished these prayers, we salute one another with the kiss of peace. Then bread and a cup of water and wine are brought to him who presides over the brethren, and he having received them, sends up praise and glory to the Father of all things, through the name of the Son and of the Holy Ghost, and gives thanks at great length (ἐπὶ πολὺ ὅση

---

[2] An excellent unabridged translation will be found in Fortescue, pp. 18 ff. To the reading of one clause alone exception may be taken, as will be pointed out in chap. xiii.

[3] Apol. 1:67.

[4] So we should probably read for εὐτόνως, which, like the rest of the text, rests on the authority of a single MS.

δύναμις αὐτ) for having been deemed worthy of these things by Him (ὑπὲρ το καταξισθαι τούτων παρ' αὐτοῦ). And after he has finished the prayers and thanksgiving all the people cry aloud, 'Amen,' which word in Hebrew signifies, 'So be it.' And after the president has finished his thanksgiving and the people have responded, those who among us are called deacons distribute the bread and wine over which the thanksgiving has been uttered to all who are present (ἡ διάδοσις καὶ μετάληψις ἀπὸ τῶν εὐχαριστηθέντων ἑκάστῳ γίνεται), and carry them to those who are absent."[5]

He then, in a very striking passage, goes on to speak of the faith of Christians concerning the Eucharist.[6] This I must needs omit, and dwell rather on the fact that we have here an outline of the liturgy of the Mass as it was celebrated, possibly in Rome, but more probably at Ephesus, in St. Justin's time. I say, more probably at Ephesus, not only because St. Justin habitually lived there, though he twice made some stay in Rome, but also because his "Dialogue," written shortly after the Apology, unquestionably has Ephesus for its scene. The service thus described consisted of the following items:

1. Lessons from the apostolical or prophetical writings.
2. A homily by the bishop on what had been read.
3. Solemn prayers, made by all in common, for the faithful at large.[7]
4. The Kiss of Peace.
5. The presentation of the bread and mixed chalice to the bishop.
6. A long thanksgiving prayer, made by the bishop, to which the people answer, Amen.

---

[5] Apol. 1:65 and 67 combined.

[6] See Fortescue, pp. 19, 21.

[7] These correspond to the deacon's litany or litanies of the Eastern liturgies, and to the series of prayers recited after the Gospel on Good Friday in the Roman rite. See vol. i. pp. 88 ff

7. The Communion.

Now having the description in view, I hardly know whether it is too much to say that, if the "Sanctus" had held its present position in Justin's time, "it is incredible that he should have passed over in silence this solemn chant, considering that he twice mentions, with some emphasis, the final response or acclamation, 'Amen'."[8] Still, the argument from silence is proverbially precarious; and although it is, I think, not without its weight in the present case, it must not, of course, be unduly pressed.

The testimony of St. Clement of Rome (c. a.d. 96–98), which at first sight might seem decisive as against the view here taken, must not, of course, be overlooked. He writes: "The Scripture says: 'Ten thousand times ten thousand waited on Him, and a thousand thousand served Him and cried: Holy, holy, holy, Lord of hosts, every creature is full of Thy glory.' Let us then also, with one mind, gathered together into one place in [obedience to our] conscience (ἐν ὁμονοίᾳ ἐπὶ τὸ αὐτὸ συναχθέντες τῇ συνειδήσει) cry to Him constantly (ἐκτενῶς) as with one voice, that we may become sharers in His great and glorious promises."[9] Now a careful examination of this passage should, I think, convince the reader of the truth of the following statements, viz.:

(1) Clement does not assert that, in his day, Christians actually chanted the "Tersanctus." In fact, he does not here make any assertion at all as to the form or forms of prayer which they used. What he does is to exhort them to pray after a certain fashion. But how? They are very earnestly or constantly to beg for a participation in the divine promises. The

---

[8] Lucas, "Fresh Light on the Early History of the Mass," in *The Month*, February, 1900. From this article much of the present chapter is taken.

[9] Clem. Rom. *Epist.* I. xxxiv. 6,7 (Funk, *Patres Apostolici*, i. 142). Cf. Fortescue, p. 13, where the hortative "pof|C7cop8v" is rendered "we cry." Funk notes no variant reading here.

Chapter IX: The Preface

angels are introduced by way of comparison. The writer urges that as they with one voice cry: "Holy, holy, holy," &c., so we as with one voice should cry out for mercy.

(2) It is by no means certain, though it is highly probable, that Clement here refers specifically to the liturgy (σύναξις). For the phrase which has been translated above, "gathered together ... in obedience to our conscience" may quite possibly mean "gathered together in conscience" or, as we might say, united by a common faith.

And (3), even if it be assumed, perhaps wrongly, that the words in question must be understood as alluding to the actual use of the "Tersanctus," and, rightly perhaps, that they have reference to the liturgy, it is at least plain enough that they give no clue at all to the position which the "Tersanctus" held, or may be supposed to have held, in the service. The point of this last remark will be clear from a document to be presently cited in which a form of "Tersanctus" occurs just before the Communion. Hence it may, I think, be safely concluded that, whatever may be the force of the argument from "the silence of Justin," it is not affected by the witness of Clement.[10]

But indeed, it is the less needful to rest the case on the testimony of St. Justin, which on this particular point may be regarded as wholly negative, because a document has been preserved which actually contains a form of Anaphora whose continuity is unbroken by the "Sanctus." This is the liturgy embodied in the "Ordinances of the Egyptian Church."[11] The

---

[10] But see Fortescue in the *Cath. Encyclop.* xiii. 432.

[11] A Latin translation of the liturgy was published so long ago as 1691, in job Leutholf's *Historia Aetheopica*, ii. 324 ff. Bunsen, in 1843, seems to have been the first to recognize its importance as representing the most primitive type of the Eucharistic prayer. But his judgment was little heeded till the original texts began to come to light. Cf. Lagarde, Aegyptiaca (1883, reprinted 1896), pp. 249 ff.; Achelis, *Die diteste Quellen des Orientalischen Kirchenrechtes* (1891) pp. 48 ff.; Brightman, *Eastern Liturgies* (1896) pp. lxxv. 189 ff.; Funk, *Didascalia et Constitutiones Apostolorum* (1905) II. xix. ff. 97 ff. Dr. Fortescue

story of the document and of its recovery is too long and complicated to be told here; but the text of the Anaphora with its interesting rubrics, deserves to be quoted in full.[12]

> "And the deacon brings the oblation to [the newly consecrated Bishop]; and he lays his hands upon the oblation, with all the presbyters, and giving thanks (εὐχαριστῶν) says thus: The Lord be with you all.
> *And all the people shall say:* With Thy spirit.
> *And he shall say:* Lift up your hearts.
> *And all the people shall say:* We have them [lifted up] to the Lord.
> *And he shall say:* Let us give thanks to the Lord.
> *And all the people shall say:* (It is) right and just.
> *And again let him pray in this manner, and say what follows according to the tradition (or institution) of the holy oblation. Then they (i.e., the presbyters), following the bishop, say the Eucharistic prayer:*
> "We give Thee thanks, O Lord, through Thy beloved Son Jesus Christ, whom in the last days Thou hast sent to us as a Saviour and Redeemer, the messenger of Thy counsel. He is the Word that is from Thee, through whom Thou madest all things by Thy will. And Thou didst send Him from Heaven into the bosom of a Virgin. He was made Flesh and was borne in her womb. And Thy Son was made known by the Holy Ghost, that He might fulfil Thy will, and that He might prepare Thy people for Thee. Stretching forth His hands He suffered, to loose the sufferers that trust in Thee.[13] Who was delivered of His own will to suffering that He might destroy death, and burst the bonds of Satan and trample on hell, and lead forth the saints and established ordinances and make known His resurrection.

---

apparently does not consider this document of importance, for he does not, I think, even mention it. Dom R. H. Connolly on the other hand (*The Tablet*, 1912, ii. 865) speaks of "the liturgy of the Ethiopic Church Order, and [that of] Serapion" as "our earliest certain texts of liturgies."

[12] The translation here given is that of J. C. Ball *(apud* Brightman, l.c.), corrected, however, from Funk's Latin version (*Didascalia*, ii. 99 f.).

[13] Funk connects "expandendo manus suas" with the preceding sentence.

Chapter IX: The Preface

Taking bread, then, He gave thanks and said: Take, eat, this is My Body which is broken for you. And in like manner the cup also and said: This is My Blood, which is shed for you; as often as ye do this, ye shall do it in remembrance of Me.

"Remembering, therefore. His death and His resurrection, we offer Thee this bread and cup, giving thanks to Thee that Thou hast made us meet to stand before Thee and do Thee priestly service. We beseech Thee therefore that Thou wouldst send Thy Holy Spirit on the oblation of this Church, and that Thou wouldst grant also to all that partake of it that it may be to them unto sanctification, that they may be filled with the Holy Spirit, and that they may be strengthened in true faith,[14] that they may extol and praise Thee in Thy Son Jesus Christ, in whom to Thee be glory and dominion in the holy Church both now and for ever, and world without end. Amen."

Now lest it should seem that undue stress is here laid on the foregoing passage, as well as on others to be hereafter quoted from documents of a similar and more or less apocryphal character, it may be well to forestall the objection that "there is no evidence to show that the liturgies or liturgical fragments embodied in such documents were ever actually in use." To this I would answer that a distinction must be drawn between the positive and the negative testimony of these compilations. For the most part no argument (except as regards provenance) can, I think, be legitimately drawn from the verbal text of any prayer which they contain.

Nor can we, apart from external evidence of a corroborative kind, be sure that any particular prayer or ceremony, even taken as a whole, which one or other of them may happen to give, represents a constitutive element of the primitive rite. The structure of these unauthentic liturgies, so far as it may happen to embody elements not demonstrably primitive, presumably represents contemporary rather than more ancient usage. Hence I cannot attach to the positive witness of the "Clementine" liturgy of the "Apostolic Constitutions," the

---

[14] "Ad confirmationem fidei in veritate.

importance which is ascribed to it by Probst, or even, in a lesser degree, by Dr. Fortescue. But if, on the other hand, it be borne in mind that, in "faked" documents, primitive texts are apt to be expanded by interpolation rather than shortened by omissions, it should be plain that what these documents omit is of far higher significance, for purposes of inferential reconstruction, than what they contain. And something of the same kind may be said of instances in which elements of the liturgy whose place has been long since fixed are found in fourth- century compilations, to occupy a different or a varying position.

To apply these principles to the case in hand, it is to me simply incredible that the rigidly simple form of the Eucharistic prayer which is found in the Ethiopic Ordinances should be of later origin than, for instance, the elaborate though singularly beautiful Anaphora of the so-called "Apostolic Constitutions," which, of course, contains the "Sanctus." Nor can I bring myself to believe that, if the "Sanctus" had already found a place in the Anaphora it would ever have lost it. Hence, without, of course, pretending that the Anaphora of the Church Ordinances is verbally identical with that which was in use in Rome in the early years of the second century, I do venture to maintain—till fresh light be thrown on the subject—the structural identity of the Eucharistic prayer of the Ordinances with the corresponding portion of the liturgy as described by St. Justin. It is a prayer in which thanks are given to God "for that He has made us meet (or deemed us worthy) to stand before Him, and to do Him priestly service," words which seem to echo a phrase of St. Justin's. Both authorities seem to me to point to a time when the unity of the "thank-prayer" ("Dankgebet," as the Germans call it) had not yet been broken by the intercalation of the "Tersanctus."

There is, indeed, one witness, of relatively late date, whose words might seem fatal to the opinion here put forward, at least in so far as this opinion relates to the time of St. Justin. Anastasius, the compiler of the "Liber Pontificalis," tells us that

Chapter IX: The Preface

Pope Xystus I (119—128) ordered that the "Sanctus" should be sung "intra actionem," *i.e.*, within the Anaphora. Now this testimony, whatever its value, cuts both ways. It implies on the one hand that (as here maintained) the "Sanctus" was inserted into the Eucharistic prayer, which hitherto had been without it. But on the other hand, it asserts that the change was made at an earlier date than that of Justin's "Apology." Hence it might seem that Justin's negative testimony must be ruled out of court. But not necessarily so. For first of all the statements of Anastasius are not in the nature of contemporary evidence, and must be accepted with caution. It is possible that he has attributed to Xystus I a change really introduced by a later Pope; for the tendency always was to antedate events rather than to postdate them. Or again, it is possible that the Papal ordinance may not have been forthwith carried into effect, except in Rome and its neighbourhood, and probable that St. Justin describes the practice of the church at Ephesus. All this, however, is somewhat problematical; and it must be admitted that the statement of the "Liber Pontificalis" is of sufficient weight to make a careful writer hesitate to affirm anything more than this, that the primitive Anaphora had no "Sanctus" "within the action," and that in the Ethiopic document which has been quoted we have either an actual or a reflected survival of the earliest usage. It should be added that in the liturgy embodied in the so-called "Testament of our Lord Jesus Christ," a fourth-century compilation of which the Syriac text was published in 1899 by Mgr. Rahmani, a short "Benedictus," followedby a short form of the "Sanctus," occurs in what was perhaps the earliest position of both, viz., not "within the action," but just before the Communion, as follows:

> "*The Deacon.* Let us earnestly beseech our Lord and God that He would grant to us to be of one mind in the Spirit.
> *The Bishop.* Grant us to be of one mind in the Holy Spirit, and heal our souls by this oblation, that we may live in Thee for ever and ever.

> The People. Amen.
> Let the people, praying, repeat the same. This done let the giving of thanks be closed after this manner.
> *[The Bishop.]* May the name of the Lord be blessed for ever.
> The People. Amen.
> *The Priest (sic).* Blessed is He that cometh in the name of the Lord, blessed is the name of His glory.
> *Let all the people say:* So be it. So be it."

And again it is directed that each of the faithful, immediately before receiving his fragment of the Sacred Host, is to say,

> "Holy, Holy, Holy Trinity unspeakable, grant me that I may receive this Body unto life and not unto condemnation."[15]

The "Testament," it may be added, though in its extant form not older than the fourth century, contains some archaic features which seem to point to an earlier date than that of the Ethiopic Ordinances, but its relation to these and other like documents cannot be said to have been satisfactorily established.[16]

Here, it is true, we have neither the full "Tersanctus" nor the full Benedictus of the later liturgies. But the use of such tentative and incomplete formulae as these would easily pave the way for the introduction of the fuller and more scriptural invocations with which we are now familiar. And the mention of Angels and Archangels, Cherubim and Seraphim, in that portion of the prayer wherein God is praised for the works of creation, would afford a ready "cue" for the placing of the invocations there, rather than at the conclusion of the Anaphora.

For the rest, it must be enough to say that, subsequently to the very early introduction of the "Sanctus" into the Anaphora, the preface (for such it now became) underwent sundry changes, especially in the Western Church. At first, like the rest

---

[15] Rahmani, *Testamentum D.N.J.C.* (1899), p. 45.

[16] Funk, *Didascalia*, II. xiii.

Chapter IX: The Preface

of the liturgy, it doubtless had a form deemed suitable for use on any day and every day of the ecclesiastical year. It contained a more or less general recital of God's benefits to man and to His chosen people, either (as in the Clementine liturgy) from creation downwards, or, more briefly, in and through the Incarnation and Passion of our Lord. In the West, but never in the East, this unchanging preface (unchanging, that is, in each local church) gave place to a great variety of more specialized and often shorter forms adapted to particular festivals or seasons.

Of such prefaces we find a considerable number in the earliest Roman Mass-books. In fact there are in the Leonianum, says Dr. Fortescue, "altogether 267, practically one for each Mass," and 54 in the Gelasianum.[17] The Gregorian book has only ten, and the reduction of the number was doubtless due to St. Gregory himself, whose activity in the matter of liturgical reform and simplification is worthily emulated by his illustrious successor. Pope Pius X, now happily reigning. To the ten Prefaces of St. Gregory, one only, that of our Lady, has since been added. And finally, as the Roman rite gradually came into all but universal use throughout the West, the old local varieties of the preface passed into comparative oblivion, to be rescued from their obscurity in modern times, and studied as liturgical relics of the past.

In conclusion, it may perchance help our devotion in hearing or celebrating Holy Mass to bear in mind that, in reciting the preface, we are engaged upon a form of prayer which—having regard to its general purport rather than to its every word—is, with the sole exception of the words of consecration, absolutely the most primitive portion of the liturgy; more primitive, indeed, than the bulk of the Canon itself.

---

[17] Fortescue, pp. 318 ff., where many interesting details are given.

CHAPTER X
THE CANON —I

THAT the Canon of the Mass, as we know it, does not exhibit throughout a primitive text of apostolic antiquity hardly needs proof. St. Gregory the Great himself ascribes the composition, or rather, as we might say, the redaction of the "prex" as he calls it, to one whom he styles "scholasticus," a scholar or learned man; one, doubtless, who in modern times would have been an important official of the Sacred Congregation of Rites.1 Nor is it to be thought that herein St. Gregory (c. 600) contradicts his predecessor. Innocent I, who, writing nearly two hundred years earlier (c. 410), might be imagined by an incautious reader to claim an apostolic origin for the very text of the liturgy. In fact, however, he is not, in the passage referred to, dealing with the text of the liturgy, but is concerned to express his disapproval of a particular practice, which he declares to be neither in accordance with primitive tradition nor sanctioned by authority.[1] [2] In his famous letter to Decentius of Gubbio he speaks of the manner of procedure ("quem morem ... in consecrandis mysteriis teneat") and of the ritual observance of the Roman Church ("Romanae ecclesiae institutiones"), which he declares are to be preferred to the "custom" of any other

---

[1] "Precem quem scholasticus composuerat" (*Epist.* ix. 12, *P.L.* lxxvii. 957). The writer of the letter uses the word "prex" in its technical or quasi-technical sense. The transition from the term "prex" to "Canon" is seen to be in process in a letter of Vigilius (c. 540) to Profuturus of Braga. He there calls it "prex canonica" (*P.L.* lxix. 18). Dates are here given, approximately, in round numbers, as being easier to remember and keep in mind.

[2] *Epist.* xxv. 3, *P.L.* xx. 552-3.

Church ("alterius quam ecclesiae Romanae consuetudinem"). That which was handed on by St. Peter ("quod a principe apostolorum Petro Romanae Ecclesiae traditum est"), is, he says, to be held fast by all; nor is anything to be added thereto without authority ("quod auctoritatem non habeat"); and the Churches of Gaul, Spain, and Africa are to follow the lead of the Roman Church ("oportet eos hoc sequi quod ecclesia Romana custodit"), to which they all owe their origin.

We need not, then, be deterred by the reverence which is due to so venerable a monument of antiquity as is the Roman Canon from investigating its structure, or from endeavouring to discover whatever can be discovered of the history of its formation. But in attempting any such inquiry, it should never be forgotten that, although the exercise of reasonable conjecture cannot be ruled entirely out of court, conjecture is, after all, admissible only when evidence, direct or indirect, is lacking; and that recourse should never be had to the conjectural method except when there is some strong positive ground for believing that there is a real problem to be solved. In the case of liturgical formulae, for instance, the mere circumstance that an erudite scholar imagines that he could arrange a series of prayers in a more logical order, or that he could better their phrasing, is not of itself a sufficient reason for setting to work on the task of conjectural reconstruction. As Mr. Brightman, for instance, has very well said: "It is easy to compare the Roman paragraphs with their parallels in the Syrian rite, and then re-arrange them in the Syrian order; but this hardly proves that they ever stood in this order."[3] Moreover, great caution is to be used lest undue weight be attached to instances of mere verbal parallelism between prayers which may be found in two or more liturgies. Such verbal parallelism of itself proves nothing, unless, indeed, it be either extensive and continuous, or of frequent recurrence, or such as to point unmistakably to some conclusion affecting the

---

[3] Brightman, *apud* Fortescue, pp. 165 f.

Chapter X: The Canon — I

very structure of the liturgy.

But to come to the point. That in the course of the three and a half centuries which elapsed between the time of St. Justin (c. 150) and that of St. Gelasius (c. 490), the Canon underwent a process of development from a primitive nucleus, and that the "scholasticus" who had left it in the form in which St. Gregory knew it must have had his predecessors in the work of revision and redaction, may be safely assumed.[4] But it should, I think, be also assumed, in default of clear evidence to the contrary, that the process of development was orderly, and was carried out under the effective control of authority. And the presumption would seem to be in favor of those who would vindicate for the Roman Canon a more or less perfect organic unity, rather than of that class of writers who imagine that they see in it a kind of patchwork, of which most of the component parts are thought to have somehow got out of their right place. For such is the impression which might be produced by the theories of Baumstark, Buchwald and Drews, as recorded by Dr. Fortescue.[5] These theories, for reasons expressed or implied above, it has not seemed necessary to discuss. They are, I cannot but think, symptomatic of a certain critical restlessness which is characteristic of our time, and which may all too easily lead even the most learned scholars altogether too far into the region of ill-founded conjecture.

Nor ought it to be to us a matter of indifference whether the Roman Canon was developed after the somewhat free and irresponsible fashion of other liturgies. Eastern and Western, now or formerly current, or whether it is the outcome of that conservative adherence to apostolic tradition, combined with the exercise of plenary authority to make such changes as might in course of time be deemed necessary or desirable, which has always been characteristic of Papal Rome.

A sober examination of the text of the Canon will, I venture

---

[4] On the external evidence available for this period see below, Chapter xiii.

[5] Fortescue, pp. 148 ff.

to hope, convince the reader that in so far as it is not actually "primitive," it is the result of a singularly well-considered redaction or series of redactions, and that its parts, with a possible and partial exception in the case of the "Mementos" for the living and the dead, belong and belonged from the outset just where they are, and nowhere else; that is to say, that the additions to the primitive text, as they were successively made, were rightly placed in their present position.

It will be well to begin with the series of intercessory and commemorative prayers which the Canon contains. They form, though not occurring in unbroken succession, a sequence of their own, and are all that, in the Roman rite, can be regarded as analogous to the "Great Intercession" of the Eastern liturgies.[6]

They are as follows:

I. "Te Igitur," &c. A commendation of the Oblata, merging into a prayer for the Pope, the Bishop, and formerly also for the Emperor, and for all the faithful.

II. "MEMENTO," &c. A prayer for particular persons ("N.N."), living, for all present, and for those on whose behalf the Holy Sacrifice is offered.

III. "COMMUNICANTES," &c. A commemoration of our Lady and the saints.[6]

---

[6] The "Great Intercession" is, I believe, so called only by modern writers. Thus Brightman (*Eastern Liturgies*, p. 578): "Intercession, The, or the Great Intercession, the prayer for the whole Church within the Anaphora," and thus distinguished from the Ektene or deacon's litany. "It is a portion of the liturgy which in its extended form is certainly not primitive; and mainly for this reason it holds widely differing positions in the several Eastern rites." This being so, the "great intercession" cannot be regarded as one of the primitive features of the liturgy of the "Apostolic Constitutions." There is, believe, no ground whatever for assuming, *a priori*, that the Roman Canon ever had a "great intercession" in any other form, so far as structure is concerned, than that which it has, or may be said to have, in the prayers specified above. To speak of it as "scattered throughout the Canon" (Fortescue, p. 329) seems rather a question-begging phrase. (Cf. R. H.

And, after the consecration:

> IV. "MEMENTO ETIAM," &c. A prayer for the deceased ("N.N.").
> V. "NOBIS QUOQUE PECCATORIBUS." A prayer for the celebrant and, perhaps, the sacred ministers, combined with a further commemoration of saints.

Now concerning these prayers, which have fed the devotion of some of us almost since, in early childhood, we were first able to toddle to church, sundry disconcerting statements are made by the most recent critics of the Roman Canon. Here are some of them:

1. We are told that, at the very outset, the word "igitur" ("therefore") is a clear indication that "Te igitur" is out of its place, and that it must originally have followed the consecration with the rest of the "great intercession."[7]

2. We are told that, because "Memento" (for the living) and "Memento etiam" for the dead manifestly in some sense belong together, therefore the second must once have followed immediately, or all but immediately, on the first, which is probably true; and moreover that both, as part of the "great intercession," must originally have followed the consecration, which is quite another matter. On this point the testimony of Innocent I (to be hereafter discussed) is, moreover, invoked.[8]

3. We are told that, grammatically speaking, "communicantes" is a participle hanging in the air, and lacking a grammatical subject.[9]

4. And finally we are told by Dr. Drews that the commemoration of certain saints in the "Nobis quoque

---

Connolly, in *The Tablet*, 1912. i. 864, 865.)

[7] Fortescue, p. 328.

[8] P. 354.

[9] P. 332.

peccatoribus" is a "reduplication" or "doublet" of the somewhat similar commemoration in the "Communicantes";[10] a doublet, as someone else has said, "derived, no doubt, from another Anaphora."

Now all these observations are, I am inclined to think, rather striking instances of a misapplication of the critical faculty. And the matter deserves very careful consideration in view of the mischief that may be done by needlessly unsettling the minds of unwary students. I would reply:

1. In the first prayer ("Te igitur") the logical nexus with the foregoing Preface is this. Having said or sung, in the preface, that "it is right and just everywhere and always to give thanks to the Father

"THROUGH CHRIST our Lord,...

"THROUGH WHOM the Angels praise Him," &c., we go on to say that: "Therefore (also)

"THROUGH CHRIST our Lord we suppliantly *beseechHim* that He would deign to bless these gifts," &c.

To the explanation of the sequence of ideas here indicated I will return presently. Meanwhile, lest there should be any difficulty in seeing a reason for the "igitur" in its present place, attention may be called to the rather numerous and remarkably similar clauses which are found here and there in the prefaces of Gallican and Mozarabic Mass-books, of which the following instances may be given:

"Te igitur... laudamus, benedicimus," &c. ("We praise Thee therefore," &c.).[11]
"Tibi ergo ... immaculatum munus offerimus," &c. ("We offer Thee therefore," &c.).[12]
"Unde supplices rogamus clementissime Pater" &c.

---

[10] Drews, apud Fortescue, p. 161.

[11] Neale and Forbes, The Gallican Liturgy, p. 142.

[12] Pp. 110, 201.

Chapter X: The Canon — I

("Wherefore, most benign Father, we beseech Thee," &c.).[13]

"*Te ergo quaesumus* ... sanctifica plebem tuam," &c. ("We beseech Thee therefore," &c.).[14]

"Tuo igitur nomini offerentes victimam ... Rogamus," &c. ("Wherefore, offering this Victim, we pray Thee," &c.).[15]

"Per eum *te igitur flagitamus* omnipotens Pater," &c. ("Through Him, therefore, we ask," &c.).[16]

Examples such as these may serve to weaken the force of Dr. Fortescue's remark (p. 328) that "it certainly does not seem that the *igitur* can be explained in its present place." The compilers of the prefaces from which these clauses are taken obviously perceived, or thought they perceived, a logical connection between the fitness of praising and thanking God and the petitions which they forthwith introduced.

But to return to the analysis given above. By means of it I have endeavoured to emphasize the fact, or what appears to me to be the fact, that the dominant idea throughout is that which is expressed by the words "through Christ our Lord." Through Him we give thanks to the Father, through Him the angels praise the Father, and therefore through Him we rightly address our petition to the Father. In this connection I would call special attention to the emphatic position of "per Christum," &c. in the "Te igitur," viz., as near as possible to the beginning of the prayer. And if it should be said that the argument implied in emphasizing the idea expressed in "per

---

[13] P. 111.

[14] P. 222.

[15] *P.L.* lxxxv. 303 (Mozarabic).

[16] *Ibid.* 188. Cf. *Dublin Review*, Jan. 1894, p. 125. These and other instances were there given in support of a suggestion which I should not now make and which need not be here repeated.

Christum," &c., is based on the "praefatio communis" or everyday preface alone, and that it could not be drawn from some of the other prefaces contained in the Roman Missal, my answer would be that the idea, though not always expressed with the same clearness as in the "praefatio communis" is always at least latent. The connection is one of thoughts rather than of words; but we may be thankful that the wording of the preface most commonly in use has been so ordered as to bring the sequence of ideas into full prominence.

But a few words of further explanation are here needed. In all other liturgies, without exception, or rather, in all those which contain the "Sanctus," one or other of the phrases of the "Sanctus" is, or originally was, "subsumed" or taken up and developed in the prayer which immediately follows it.[17] Of this the most obvious example is "Vere sanctus, vere benedictus" ("truly holy and blessed indeed is He," &c.) of the Gallican rite. It might have been expected, then, that in the earliest form of the Roman Canon some similar phrase would be found, whereby the continuity of the Eucharistic prayer (momentarily interrupted by the "Sanctus") should be resumed and carried on. But if only we look a little closely into the matter it will be seen from what has been said above that the Canon as we actually know it has its "subsumption," the phrase and idea taken up being drawn, however, not from the "Sanctus" itself, but, as has just been pointed out, from the body of the preface.[18]

It is true, of course, and may indeed be described as obviously true, that the Mementos for the living and the dead ("Memento," &c., and "Memento etiam," &c.) do in a sense belong together. But, on the assumption, to be hereafter justified, that these two prayers are in the nature of insertions

---

[17] *e.g.* Brightman, pp. 19 (Clementine), 51 (Syrian), 125 (Egyptian), 324 (Byzantine).

[18] That the Roman Mass once had a "Vere sanctus" seems to me highly probable. The point will be discussed elsewhere. Meanwhile we are here concerned with the Canon as it stands.

into a pre-existing text, that they have been transferred to their present places from the offertory, and that in their original position the Mementos for the dead probably followed immediately on that for the living, one or other of various reasons may be suggested for their separation.[19] Probst suggests that they were separated in order that the Memento for the dead might not be brought into unduly close connection with the commemoration of the saints, as was the case in some at least of the early liturgies. Indeed, a western example of the confusion hence arising occurs in the Stowe Missal; and it was plainly of importance that it should be avoided.[20] Or again, it may have been thought more appropriate that the prayer for the dead should follow rather than precede the commemoration of our Lord's own passion and death. Or, lastly, as a mere matter of convenience, it may have seemed well to divide the otherwise somewhat lengthy reading of the diptychs. For there can be no doubt that the names of the persons prayed for (represented by the "N.N." of the Mementos as we know them), were originally read aloud. This last reason would have more force if, as may possibly be the case, the custom had crept in by which the celebrant continued the recital of the Canon while the names were being read. In this case the separation of the Mementos would be precisely analogous to the separation of the Benedictus, as sung by the choir, from the Sanctus, the singing of the Benedictus being usually held over, as we all know, till after the consecration.

In order to explain the apparent lack of a subject to support

---

[19] Whether the separation took place contemporaneously with the transfer, or subsequently thereto, is a point which, in the present state of our knowledge, cannot, I think, be determined. For instances of "Memento defunctorum" following immediately on "Memento vivorum" within the Canon itself, see Ebner, *Quellen, usw.* pp. 405 ff. These instances Ebner regards as reminiscences of the older usage, when both Mementos had their place in the offertory.

[20] Probst, *Abendl. Messe*, p. 165, MacCarthy, pp. 216 ff. On the "detachability" of the Mementos cf. Cabrol, apud Fortescue, pp. 167 f.

"Communicantes," it is only necessary to bear in mind that, as has been already pointed out, the two Mementos were originally the prayers which accompanied the reading of the diptychs, which no one can suppose to have been a quite primitive custom.[21] Hence we are not, or ought not to be, greatly surprised to find that, in the Roman Canon, the *Memento* for the living breaks the grammatical sequence of the prayers between which it has been inserted. In other words, the Memento for the living is to be considered as, in a manner, parenthetic. And the same is to be said of the Memento for the dead, though in this case there is no such obvious interruption of the logical sequence, and no grammatical irregularity. It may be added that the parenthetic character of the Mementos may be more readily understood and recognized if we remember that, at least down to the end of the fourth century, the diptychs were read by the deacon. This is plain from the explicit testimony of St. Jerome, who bitterly complains that deacons in his day curried favor with the rich by not only reading their names, but proclaiming the amount of their offerings.[22] Now, the parenthetic character of the Memento being once understood, it ought to be clear enough to any one who has not a special theory to support, that "Communicantes" does not, after all, lack a subject, which is supplied by the prayer "Te igitur." The constructionis: "Offerimus... communicantes," *i.e.*, "We offerThee these gifts ... in communion with" our Lady and the saints.

There remains one other point to be noticed in connection with the hypothesis, now in favor, that the "great intercession,"

---

[21] The rubric "Super diptitia," or " s. dyptitia," or "s. dypticia," is found in three sacramentaries described by Ebner (pp. 105, 213, 214), and the first of them has, before "istis et omnibus," the further rubric: "Post lectionem."

[22] "Publiceque in ecclesiis diaconus recitet (? recitat) offerentium nomina: tantum offert illa, tantum ille pollicitus est; placentque sibi ad plausum populi" (In Ezech. vi. 18; *P.L.* xxv. 175). How soon this abuse was abolished and the deacons relieved of the office of reading the diptychs, we do not know.

Chapter X: The Canon — I

the very existence of which, at any period in the development of the Roman rite, is more than problematical, once had its rightful place after the consecration. If the Memento for the living, and, as the critics will have it, the "Communicantes" also, had immediately preceded the Memento for the dead and the "Nobis quoque peccatoribus," we should have to account for the awkwardness of a double commemoration of the saints with its two parts in close proximity.[23] It is, indeed, this very awkwardness—arising, not from the present position of the prayers, but from possibly ill-advised attempts at reconstruction—which has led some critics, and formerly led the present writer, to imagine that the commemoration of the saints had been duplicated from two distinct and originally independent sources, which is the last of the four criticisms cited above. A vain imagination, seeing that, as Dr. Fortescue has pointed out, the second list of saints ("John, Stephen," &c.), so far from being a "doublet" of the first, is manifestly intended to supplement it.[24]

There is, then, nothing in the intercessory portions of the Canon to shake the conviction that, as I hope to show more clearly in the following chapters, the "scholasticus" of St. Gregory's letter is to be credited with a very perfect piece of work; a compilation, no doubt, in great measure, from earlier and more primitive sources, but deserving to be regarded rather as a beautiful mosaic than as a specimen of patchwork to be picked to pieces by the scissors of the modem critic.

---

[23] Viz. the "Communicantes" itself and the words, "cum Joanne, Stephano" &c. in the "Nobis quoque."

[24] Fortescue, p. 355. For some particulars, see chap, xv., where a real case of reduplication, as between the Ordinary and the Canon of the Mass, will be pointed out.

CHAPTER XI
THE CANON - II

HAVING analyzed, as regards its structure and the mutual relations of its constituent elements, that part of the Canon of the Mass which consists of intercessory and commemorative prayers, some of which precede and others follow the consecration, we have now to consider what remains of this central portion of the Mass. We shall then be in a position to inquire whether it affords any indications by which we may, with some degree of probability, determine the steps by which its primitive nucleus was, by successive augmentations, brought to its present form.

After the "Communicantes," which, be it observed, ends with the "clausula"—"Per Christum Dominum nostrum. Amen," the "Hanc igitur" resumes the thoughts which have been expressed in the "Te igitur." It echoes the first part of the "Te igitur" in the words "Hanc igitur oblationem ... accipias" ("Receive, then, this offering"), and it may perhaps be said to reflect its last clause ("et omnibus orthodoxis"—"and all orthodox believers," &c.) in the words "servitutis nostrae ... *et cunctae familiae tuae*" ("which we Thy servants *together with Thy whole family make* to Thee"). Gifts and givers, says Probst, are alike commended to God's mercy. And then, on behalf of those who have made their offerings at the Mass, and of all the faithful, a threefold boon is asked; peace, God's own peace, in this life ("diesque nostros in *tua* pace disponas"), and in the next world deliverance from eternal damnation, and union with the company of the elect.¹ In this last clause we have, of course, an echo of the "Communicantes." This prayer is likewise closed—and this is a point to be noted for future reference—with the words "per Christum Dominum nostrum. Amen."

In the prayer "Quam oblationem" we beg that God will bless the gifts (*i.e.*, the bread and wine), that He will now regard them as inviolably dedicated to His service, that He will ratify the bond thus entered into as between Himself and the offerer, that He will accept them as part of our reasonable service ("benedictam, adscriptam, ratam, rationabilem acceptabilemque facere digneris"); and all this to the end that on our behalf they may be changed and may become the Body and Blood of His most dear Son our Lord Jesus Christ ("ut nobis Corpus et Sanguis fiat dilectissimi Filii tui Domini nostri Jesu Christi"). Here it is to be noted that the prayer has no "conclusion" in the technical sense of the term. Nor is there any need, so far as mere grammar is concerned, for a stop here; though reverence may suggest a suspensive pause before "Qui pridie quam pateretur" ("Who, on the day before He suffered"), which forthwith introduces the words of institution and consecration.

Concerning the words of consecration there are several points to be noted. First of all the Roman Canon, followed herein by the Ambrosian, Gallican and old Spanish rites, substitutes the words: "Qui pridie quam pateretur" ("Who, the day before He suffered") for St. Paul's "in qua nocte tradebatur"² ("on the night wherein He was betrayed"), which words of the Apostle are retained by all the Eastern liturgies without exception. The use of "Qui pridie," or, as an occasional Gallican variant, "Ipse enim pridie," to introduce the words of consecration is one of the chief among the characteristic

---

¹ Cf. Probst, *Abendl. Messe*, pp. 166 f. 249. Probst, however, would connect the "Hanc igitur" more closely with the Memento than I should be disposed to do.

² 1 Cor. 11:23.

features which distinguish all the Western from all the Eastern rites.³ Even the Mozarabic, which now has "in qua nocte," &c., unquestionably once had, like the Roman, Ambrosian and Gallican, the introductory formula "Qui pridie." The substitution of this Western form for that of St. Paul's account of the institution, the "Liber Pontificalis" ascribes to Alexander I (c. 110), nor does there seem to be any good reason for doubting the correctness of the attribution.⁴ Even were it only approximately true, it would show that already in the early days of the second century the Popes were solicitous about the very words of at least the central portion of what is now—but was not yet called—the Canon.

Moreover, the Roman Canon makes four additions to the words in which the institution of the Holy Eucharist is recorded in the New Testament. In these, likewise, it would seem that the Gallican rite conformed to the Roman type. It is, indeed, impossible to speak with full confidence on this point. For, except in the "Missa cottidiana Romensis," which, of course, has the Roman Canon, the Gallican Masses give only the initial words "Qui pridie," omitting the rest. It is probable, however, that if this had been other than what follows in the Roman Canon, some indication of the discrepancy would have survived.⁵

1. The phrase, occurring twice, *i.e.*, before each consecration, "in sanctas ac venerabiles manus suas" ("into His sacred and venerable hands").

---

[3] Lucas in *Dublin Review,* 1894, i. 115; Cagin, Paleographie Musicale, v. 55. On this and the statement which follows in the text see chap. xvi.

[4] "Hic (sc. Alexander) passionem Domini miscuit in precatione sacerdotum, quando missae celebrantur" (*P.L.* cxxvii. 1145-7; Duchesne i. 127, with a variant reading). These words are commonly, and rightly, recognized as having reference to the form "Qui pridie." Duchesne (*l.c.*) speaks, as it seems to me, very inaccurately (c.f. *Dublin Review, l.c. note* 1), and Cagin (*l.c.* note 1), rather hesitatingly on the point.

[5] The text of *M. cottidiana* may be found in *P.L.* lxxii. 454, and, with many interpolations, in the Stowe Missal.

2. The clause, "elevatis oculis in coelum ad te Deum Patrem suum omnipotentem" ("lifting up His eyes towards heaven, to Thee O God His almighty Father").

3. The italicized words in "hunc praeclarum calicem" ("this most excellent chalice").

4. (The words "aeterni" and "mysterium fidei" ("the mystery of faith") in the consecration of the chalice.

Now, considering the emphasis laid by Innocent I on "the tradition delivered to the Roman Church by St. Peter, the prince of the apostles," and considering, too, the entire absence of these or any corresponding phrases in the Eastern rites, otherwise so prone to enlargements and expansion, it is perhaps not altogether rash to surmise the possibility that we have here some far-off reminiscence of the very words of the Apostle himself.[6]

As everyone who has any acquaintance with the subject is aware, in all the Eastern liturgies, except the early Ethiopic, the words of consecration are followed by an "Anamnesis" or "prayer of remembrance." To this prayer, as regards both name and place, occasion is given by our Lord's precept, following immediately on the words of institution: "This do ye in remembrance of Me." Of course the Gallican liturgy likewise had its anamnesis, though in too many of the prayers which occupy this position in the surviving Gallican Mass-books, the idea of remembrance is either obscured or has been altogether ousted. Not so, as we know very well, in the Roman Canon, which has its singularly perfect and beautiful anamnesis, viz., the prayer "Unde et memores." It contains not a superfluous word, and is, moreover, full of echoes of the earlier part of the Canon. The prayer runs thus:

---

[6] Cf. an excellent article by the late Dr. J. R. Gasquet, in the *Dublin Review*, July 1890, pp. 86-87. He lays stress, inter alia, on the order in which the names of the Apostles occur in "Communicantes," as possibly indicating the existence of a Roman tradition concerning these chosen followers of our Lord, independent of the lists in the Gospels and Acts.

"Wherefore, O Lord, we Thy servants and Thy holy people, remembering the blessed passion of the same Christ Thy Son, as also His resurrection from the dead and His glorious ascension into heaven, offer to Thy most excellent Majesty, of Thy gifts and boons, a pure Host, a holy Host, a spotless Host, the holy Bread of eternal life and the Chalice of everlasting salvation."

It is plain that the idea of remembrance is here closely conjoined with that of oblation or sacrifice, and that the sacrificial idea is expressed in terms which recall those of the "Te igitur" and the "Hanc igitur." But, together with points of similarity, a sharp contrast, alike in affirmation and in point of view, is here to be observed. The text deserves the closest scrutiny.

First, then, the words "nos servi tui, sed et plebs tua sancta" ("we Thy servants as also Thy holy people") are manifestly an echo of "servitutis nostrae sed et *cunctae familiae tuae*" ("of our servantship as also of *all Thy family*") occurring in the "Hanc igitur"; and the phrases "de tuis donis ac datis" ("of Thy gifts and boons"), and "hostiam puram, hostiam sanctam, hostiam immaculatam" ("a pure Host, a holy Host, a spotless Host") no less obviously recall the similar but more condensed expressions of the "Te igitur"—"haec dona, haec munera, haec sancta sacrificia illibata" ("These gifts, these presents, this holy and unspotted sacrifice"). When, however, it is said that in "Unde et memores" we find "echoes" of "Hanc igitur," the statement must be understood of the text as it now stands. But it is obvious that if there should be independent grounds for thinking that "Hanc igitur" is by one stage later than "Unde et memores" in the process of the formation of the Canon, then it must be said that "Hanc igitur," when it was inserted in the more primitive text, was very skilfully so fashioned as to refer back to the "Te igitur" and forwards to "Unde et memores."

But now mark the contrast, in idea and in expression, between the prayers that precede and those which follow the consecration. Before the consecration, the oblata, plain bread and wine, mere material things, are our offerings, God's gifts indeed (if such be the true force of the word "dona"), but still ours to give back to Him ("munera"), and on these our offerings we beg a blessing. But after the consecration they have been transmuted into something very different from mere material objects; they have become "the bread of eternal life and the chalice of everlasting salvation."[7] They are ours indeed, and they are offered once more; but they are no longer ours in the same sense in which they were ours when they were only bread and wine, the property of an individual, which he might have turned to some other use. They are now, in a far higher sense than before, God's gifts ("de *Luis* donis ac datis") but these gifts are now available for no other use than that of sacrifice. They are no longer in the nature of personal property which might have been otherwise disposed of. They have passed out of our control; in the very act and moment of consecration they have been offered to the Eternal Father by our great High Priest, Jesus Christ; and all that we can now do is to unite our intention with His self-offering.

Accordingly, in the following prayer, "Supra quae," God is asked to regard the offering not merely as "acceptable" (the word used before the consecration, in "Quam oblationem") but as "accepted," even as were those of Abel, Abraham and Melchisedech, and (as is implied by the words "sanctum sacrificium immaculatam hostiam") in a higher sense and with a fuller measure of acceptance.[8]

It may indeed be objected that we find the expression "accepta habere" occurring already in the "Te igitur," but the fact that this is so only serves to emphasize, instead of

---

[7] "Offerimus temporalia, aeterna recipimus," says an old writer.

[8] The words "sanctum sacrificium," &c., are said to have been added by St. Leo the Great (c. 450). So the "Liber Pontificalis" (Duchesne, i. 239, apud Fortescue, p. 137). The statement does not occur in P.L. cxxviii. 299 ff, the only edition at present accessible to me.

obscuring, the phraseological difference just noted. For in the "Te igitur" we are still in the region and domain of material objects. As such we there asked that the offerings might be "held for accepted." But in the "Quam oblationem" we beg that, by virtue of the consecration, they may be rendered "acceptable" on, so to say, a higher plane. And on this higher plane we ask in "Unde et memores" that the consecrated elements may be "held for accepted." It is only in the light of the Catholic dogma of transubstantiation that the words of the Canon can be fully appreciated or even rightly understood.

Then in the prayer "Supplices te rogamus," we ask, using a bold and dramatic figure of speech to express a sublime truth, that by the ministry of an Angel, the sacrifice may be carried to the heavenly altar, the altar of which we read in the Apocalypse, and there presented to the Divine Majesty; to the end that all who from this material altar (which the celebrant here kisses) shall receive the Body and Blood of Christ may be filled with all heavenly blessings and graces. Here follows, again be it noted, the conclusion: "Per eumdem Christum Dominum nostrum. Amen."

Concerning the Memento for the dead and the "Nobis quoque peccatoribus," nothing need here be said beyond noting that each of these prayers has the "clausula," "Per Christum," &c., but that the second of them has no "Amen." Instead of "Amen," there follows an expansion or enlargement of the "Per Christum," &c., in the following terms: "Through whom, O Lord, Thou dost ever create, hallow, quicken, bless, and bestow on us all these good things."

But what are "all these good things"? There seems to be little doubt that these words originally had reference, inclusively but not exclusively, to the offerings, other than those of the bread and wine for the sacrifice, which in early days were made after the Gospel; and that they continued to have this application to material objects, at least inclusively, when, far down into the Middle Ages, a lamb was brought to be blessed on St. Agnes' day, January 21st, the first-fruits of the harvest on Ascension Day, and those of the vintage on the feast of St. Xystus, August 6th.[9]

And then the theme with which the preface began ("We thank Thee through Christ our Lord") and ended ("The angels praise Thee, and we with them, through Christ our Lord"), the theme which the Canon carried on from its commencement ("We beseech Thee through Christ our Lord"), and which is echoed again and again in the conclusion ("per Christum," &c.) of precisely five of its prayers,—this theme receives its final and comprehensive development in what may deservedly and with all reverence be called the solemn finale of the Canon—

"Through Him, and with Him, and in Him is to Thee, God the Father almighty, in the unity of the Holy Ghost, all honour and glory

"For ever and ever.[10] R. Amen."

Here, as we all know, at "per omnia saecula saeculorum," the priest raises his voice, and the response is made by the choir, or, in a Low Mass, by the clerk. This is the final "Amen" at the close of the great Eucharistic prayer, to which St. Justin, in his description of the Mass as celebrated in the second century, so pointedly calls attention.[11]

---

[9] Or, as we learn from contemporary witnesses, on a later day in case a dull summer had delayed the ripening of the grapes (Bona, II. xiv. 5; cf. Fortescue, p.358).

[10] Cf. Rom. 11:36; 1 Cor. 8:6.

[11] See above, chap. ix.

The Holy Mass

CHAPTER XII
THE CANON - III

Have already expressed the conviction that there is no sufficient ground for the opinion, too confidently held as it seems to me by some modern writers, that in the interval of about three centuries and a half which elapsed between the time of St. Justin (c. 150) and that of Gelasius (c. 490) the Roman Canon underwent a wholesale transposition of its parts, with the result that it must now be regarded as a patchwork of somewhat ill-assorted and ill- arranged fragments. All that we know of the actual history of the liturgy during the period in question, though that is little enough, should, I think, lead us to believe that in Rome, or at any rate in the principal churches of the holy city, no change was ever made in the text of the Canon without Papal authority, and that the Popes themselves were, to say the least, slow to make or to authorize such changes. That it was far otherwise in regions where, under the circumstances of the times, the authority of the Pope in liturgical matters could not be effectively exercised, may be seen from the vagaries of the early Gallican Mass-books, one of which has a Mass entirely composed, down to the "Qui pridie," in verse. And that the abuse of unauthorized interpolations long survived the adoption, in substance, of the Roman rite, appears, to cite no other instances, from the text of the Stowe Missal as re-cast by Moel Caich, and from a strong passage in

the "Micrologus."[1] There is obviously a very wide difference between an orderly and gradual expansion carried out under authority, and a more or less subversive and revolutionary—not to say arbitrary—transposition of the principal parts of the Canon. That augmentations, transpositions, substitutions, all made by authority, were possible, we know from what we are told of the liturgical changes carried out, on a very restricted scale, by St. Gregory the Great. But no change under any one of these three heads must be assumed to have taken place unless there are really strong grounds for believing that it actually did take place. For such indications we have now to seek; and the following I believe to be a complete list of them:

1. It has been already seen that the Memento for the living so interrupts the grammatical sequence as between "Te igitur" and "Communicantes," that it may fairly be regarded as an inserted paragraph. This is altogether in accordance with what we should expect; for a prayer for the Pope and prelates and the faithful in general, such as we have in the "Te igitur," would by the nature of things have found a place in the liturgy long before the custom arose of making public mention of particular persons (benefactors, &c.) other than those who were entitled ex efficio to be thus named. And the same, mutatis mutandis, would hold good of the Memento for the dead, which must also have been inserted, or substituted for an earlier form of more general import, in a preexisting text. The circumstance that the two Mementos are (apparently) connected by "etiam" ("also"), and that the first lacks the "conclusion" ("per Christum," &c.), which the second has, must also be taken into account. It has been already assumed, in chapter x., that the Mementos were, probably at some time in the fourth century,

---

[1] Cf. *P.L.* cxxxviii. 876; MacCarthy, pp. 140-233; Probst, *op. Cit.* 43; and *P.L.* cli. 985. The "Micrologus" is a liturgical treatise (c. 1050-1100) of uncertain authorship, unless indeed Don G. Morin's ascription of the tract to Bernold of Constance is to be accepted or established *(Revue Benedictine* vin. 335 ff. apud Fortescue p. 195 note).

transferred from the offertory. This assumption appears to me to be justified by the undoubted fact that in the Gallican rite, and therefore by inference in the earlier Roman rite from which the Gallican was derived, the "Nomina" were proclaimed just before the prayer which corresponds to the Roman secreta.[2] The fact that "Communicantes" has its own "conclusion" is an indication, I believe, that if the two Mementos were thus transferred, "Communicantes" was not transferred with them, and that it stands on a quite different footing.

Having in view the primitive continuity of the Eucharistic prayer, there is, I think, a presumption to the effect that those sections of the Canon which end with "Amen" are of a somewhat less early date than those in which the transition to the section next following is made without any break in the sense. This consideration would lead us to believe, what is obviously probable on other grounds, that the prayer "Communicantes" does not belong to the fundamental stratum of the Canon. And it seems entirely reasonable to suppose that "Hanc igitur," which also has its "Amen," and which resumes "Te igitur" after the break caused by "Memento" and "Communicantes," had no place in the Canon until this break had been made by at least the latter of these two prayers. As for "Nobis quoque," which has the "conclusion" ("per Christum," &c.), though not the "Amen," at first sight it undoubtedly seems to postulate the previous Memento, and consequently to be of contemporary or possibly of later introduction. For to connect it with the end of the preceding prayer, "Supplices," involves the awkwardness of coupling, by means of the word "also," two clauses both of which are in the first person plural. In other words, it seems strange, after praying that "those of us" who shall have received the Holy Sacrament may be abundantly blessed, forthwith to ask that "to us also" (as well as to "those of us" who shall have communicated) may be granted the

---

[2] On the relation between the Gallican and the Roman liturgies, see chap. xvi.

fellowship of the saints. Yet we may well learn caution from the fact that several MSS. of the Gregorianum have no Memento for the dead at this point.[3] For, whatever the explanation of the fact may be, it at least serves to show that no incongruity was perceived in joining "Nobis quoque" to the end of "Supplices." The explanation would seem to be that "quotquot sumpserimus" ("those of us who shall have received," &c.) is regarded as equivalent to a clause in the third person plural ("those who shall have received"), while the "we" or "us" of the "Nobis quoque" has reference to the celebrant only, and is thus, equivalently, in the first person singular. I am confirmed in thinking that "Nobis quoque" is contemporary with "Communicantes" by the manifestly supplementary character of the list of saints who are enumerated in the second of the two prayers. To this point I shall have occasion to recur in Chapter xv.

Lastly, the "Amen" at the end of the prayer "Supplices," indicating as it does that the primitive continuity of the Eucharistic prayer has here again been broken, gives some confirmation to a surmise, resting on independent grounds, that an "Epiklesis" or invocation of the Holy Spirit once had its place here, and that "Supplices," &c., has been substituted for it.

The question as to the Epiklesis is too large to be discussed here, and such a discussion hardly falls within the scope of this book. Since, however, it is commonly and with high probability held that the Roman rite once included an invocation of the Holy Spirit similar to those which are found in the Eastern liturgies, it seems desirable that a brief statement on the subject should find its place here. The facts would seem to be, roughly

---

[3] Ebner, *Quellen, usw.* pp. 405 ff.

speaking, as follows:

1. The epiklesis in its fully developed form was an invocation to the Holy Spirit to change the elements of bread and wine into the Body and Blood of Christ.

2. The epiklesis, at least in this form, was almost certainly not primitive. Indeed the earliest extant testimony seems to indicate that even so late as the end of the third century this prayer was still in process of formation and fixation. Thus Serapion's liturgy has, after the words of institution, an invocation, not to the Holy Spirit but to the Divine Word, to "make the bread His Body,"[4] &c. On the other hand an ancient liturgical fragment recently discovered among the ruins of the monastery of Balyeh, near Siout, in Upper Egypt, and described in great detail by Dom P. Puniet, has, before the words of institution, an invocation of the Holy Spirit, who is prayed "to make the bread the Body of our Lord and Saviour Jesus Christ."[5] Whether Father Puniet is right in his conjecture that this was the original position of the epiklesis in the Alexandrian rite I will not venture to affirm. But the very fact that the epiklesis did not at first uniformly hold the same position, seems to me to point to the conclusion that it was in the nature of an addition to the primitive Anaphora. And this conclusion is confirmed by the Epiklesis of the Ethiopic Ordinances. Here it follows the words of institution, but its purport is to implore that the Holy Spirit would render the offerings profitable for holiness to those who receive them.[6] So that the diversities of usage concerned, (a) the Divine Person invoked, (b) the nature of the petition, and (c) its place in the liturgy.

---

[4] Funk, *Didascalia*, ii. 174 ff. Rauschen, *Florilegium Patristicum*, vii. 28, cites from a fragment of St. Athanasius a statement that, at the time of "the great prayers," "the Word descends on the bread, and it becomes the Body" of Christ.

[5] Puniet, in the *Record of the XIXth Eucharistic Congress*, pp. 383 ff.

[6] Funk, *Didascalia*, ii. 100.

Chapter XII: The Canon — III

3. In some form, and in some position, usually after the words of institution, it would seem to have become common to all liturgies, at an early stage of their development.

4. Its insertion, or perhaps we should rather say, the position which it finally came to hold, may possibly have been suggested by the appropriateness of introducing, after the "remembrance" of the resurrection and ascension, some reference to the work of the Holy Spirit.

5. The occurrence of the verbs ἀναδεíκνυναι and ἀποφάινειν ("to show") in sundry forms of the epiklesis, may perhaps be thought to point back to a time when the office which the Holy Spirit was implored to fulfil was that of manifesting to us the divine gift rather than that of effecting the consecration. It is, however, clear beyond dispute that, whatever its original purport may have been, the epiklesis, in course of time, came to be commonly understood as a petition that the Holy Spirit would effect the change of the elements. And the same character it plainly has in some at least of the Western examples which survive or are preserved in Gallican and Mozarabic prayers "post Pridie." And since the persuasion that the consecration was effected by the epiklesis involved, or was commonly understood to involve, a denial of the consecrating efficacy of the words of institution, the Council of Florence, in 1439, explicitly defined the sufficiency of the words of institution to effect the transubstantiation of the elements, and condemned any error to the contrary. In view, then, of the manifest danger of such errors, it is plain that there was, at a much earlier date, good and sufficient reason for substituting another prayer for the epiklesis, or changing the invocation into the form ("Supplices te rogamus," &c.), which it now has in the Roman rite. In view of the fact that Gelasius, in a fragment of a letter which has been preserved, makes an explicit reference to an epiklesis as then in use, it is at least

possible that it was he who made the substitution or change.[7]

The following scheme will indicate what appear to me to have been, most probably, the successive steps of a gradual and orderly development of the Roman Canon from its nucleus. In the first column it has seemed well to give, besides the initial words, enough to indicate the general meaning and purport of the several prayers.

---

[7] On the whole subject see Fortescue, art. "Epiklesis" in the *Cath. Encycl.* v. 502 f., where abundant references will be found.

Chapter XII: The Canon — III

First Stage.	Augments (I)	Augments (II)
TE IGITUR ... rogamus ut ... sacrificia ... accipias.... quae offerimus pro Ecclesia ... Papa ... fidelibus		MEMENTO (pro vivis)
	COMMUNICANTES, &c. HANC IGITUR, &c.	
QUAM OBLATIONEM ... acceptabilem facere digneris, ut Corpus et Sanguis fiat D.N.J.C. QUI PRIDIE quam pateretur, &c. (sequuntur verba consecratoria). Haec quotiescumque, &c. UNDE ET MEMORES ... passionis ... resurrectiones ascensionis offerimus ... panem vitae ... et calicem salutis. SUPRA QUAE ... respicere digneirs ... [eaque] accepta habere ... [?EPIKLESIS]		
	SUPPLICES, &c.	
		MEMENTO ETIAM (pro defunctis).
	NOBIS QUOQUE.	
PER QUEM haec omnia ... benedicas &c. PER IPSUM, &c. AMEN.		

While however it has seemed desirable on the one hand to vindicate the Roman Canon from the charge of being a mere patchwork of materials not too skillfully pieced together, and while it has seemed worthwhile to make an attempt, guided by definite indications, to trace its orderly growth from an assignable nucleus, it must on the other hand be admitted that even this nucleus, or rather that portion of it which precedes the consecration (*i.e.*, the "Te igitur" and "Quam oblationem") is not in the highest sense primitive. Neither St. Justin's description, nor the rudimentary liturgy of the Ethiopic Church Ordinances, give any hint of intercessory petitions as forming part of the great Eucharistic prayer. Or rather, there is no hint of any other petition except that which in the Ethiopic form of this prayer is, as has been seen, addressed to the Holy Spirit, praying Him to make the Holy Eucharist efficacious for salvation and sanctification to those who received it. In the primitive liturgy the intercessory petitions would seem to have all had their place before the commencement of the great "act" of thanksgiving and consecration. Thus, when St. Justin describes the intercessory prayers which follow the lessons as "put up" by the congregation (and thereby distinguished from the Eucharistic prayer which is put up by the celebrant alone), we must suppose that the petitions formed a kind of litany, to the successive clauses of which the people responded.

The statement just made about St. Justin's testimony requires perhaps a word of justification, the more so as on this point I cannot see my way to agree with Dr. Fortescue. The facts, as pointed out by Dom R. H. Connolly are these.[8] St. Justin uses the following expressions (and none other) in describing the great Eucharistic prayer offered by the celebrant after the people have "sent up their petitions."

1. He "sends up *praise* and *glory* and *thanksgiving*,"[9]
2. After he has finished the *prayers* and *thanksgiving*, the people answer: "Amen."[10]

---

[8] Connolly in *The Tablet*, 1912, i. 864 B.

[9] Apol. 1:65 (abridged).

[10] *Ibid.* "Immediately afterwards, referring back" to the praise and thanksgiving previously mentioned, "he describes them as 'the prayers and the thanksgiving' " (Connolly).

3. He "sends up *prayers* together with *thanksgiving*."[11]

Father Connolly is surely right in contending that the only "prayers" here referred to "are prayers of praise, not of intercession." And even were it to be contended that the word " prayers " must needs imply intercession, it at least cannot be urged that the phrases "prayer and thanksgiving" and "prayers together with thanksgiving" imply that the thanksgiving came first, and was *followed*, as in the "Clementine" liturgy, by the alleged intercessory supplication. This is a point well and strongly urged by Father Connolly, who seems to be abundantly justified in rendering "εὐχὰς ὁμοίως καὶ εὐχαριστίας"—"prayers and *likewise* thanksgivings," i.e., "prayers *together with* thanksgiving," and not, as Dr. Fortescue translates the phrase,—"prayers in the same way [i.e., in the same way as the people had done] and thanksgiving." Father Connolly has, I think, made it clear beyond reasonable doubt that it is a mistake to give to "ὁμοίως καὶ" a retrospective meaning.

Nor is it from St. Justin and the Church Ordinances alone that we may draw a probable conclusion to the effect that "Te igitur" and "Quam oblationem" have displaced, in the Roman rite, an earlier form of what, for convenience may henceforth be spoken of as the "Post Sanctus." It has already been observed that the "Sanctus," with its accompanying "Benedictus," did not, on its first introduction into the Anaphora, so entirely break the continuity of the latter as at first sight it seems to do in the Mass as we know it. In every extant liturgy which contains the Sanctus and Benedictus, with the sole exception of the Roman and Romanized Ambrosian, the prayer which immediately follows forthwith takes up and develops, in one way or another, the words of the acclamation. Thus, in the early Gallican rite, the "Post Sanctus" most commonly, though by no means invariably, begins with the words "Vere sanctus,

---

[11] Apol. 1:67 ("preces *una cum* gratiarum actionibus," Rauschen).

vere benedictus" *(i.e.,* "Holy indeed, and truly blessed," &c.), and proceeds without interruption to the "Qui pridie." The point is of sufficient importance to deserve illustration by means of a typical example from a Gallican Mass. The Mass, it will be observed, is of the Epiphany.

COLLECTIO POST SANCTUS.

"Holy indeed and truly blessed is our Lord Jesus Christ who, to make manifest His Divine generation, on this day bestowed on the world these wonders of His majesty, to wit, the star which He showed to the Magi, the conversion—after an interval of time—of water into wine, and the hallowing of the waters of Jordan by His baptism.

"Who, the day before He suffered," &c.[12]

The very form of this particular prayer is enough to illustrate the truth that in the Gallican liturgy the "post Sanctus" varied—as did also the "post Pridie" or "post Mysterium"—with the season and the feast. It is not suggested that this was ever the case in Rome. But bearing in mind what I cannot but regard as the all but demonstrable fact of the distinctively Roman origin of the Gallican rite, and taking account also of the plainly analogous yet no less distinctively dissimilar character of the "post Sanctus" in the Eastern liturgies, it seems to me impossible to resist the conclusion that the original Roman "post Sanctus" must have closely resembled the Gallican; and that the probabilities are almost overwhelmingly in favor of the hypothesis that it began with the very words "Vere sanctus, vere benedictus."[13] For it is not

---

[12] *P.L.* lxxii. 243.

[13] *Dublin Review,* Jan. 1894, pp. 121-122; Cagin, *Paleogr. Musicale,* v. 71. All the liturgies agree in taking up the words of the Sanctus, but they do so in characteristically different ways. The "Clementine" and Byzantine have, in substance: "Holy indeed and all-holy art Thou ... and Holy is Thy Only-begotten Son" (Brightman, pp. 19, 324, 385,403). The Antiochene family give to the Sanctus an emphatically Trinitarian sense, thus, in substance: "Holy

easy to suppose that the churches of Lombardy, Spain, Gaul and Ireland would all have independently hit upon this particular and characteristic form of words; whereas if the phrase "Vere sanctus, vere benedictus" were of Roman origin, its use throughout the Western chinch would find its most obvious explanation.[14] The one weak point in the argument, merely as regards this highly specialized verbal formula, lies in the fact that the "post Sanctus" in the Gallican books does not, after all, invariably begin with the words "Vere sanctus."[15]

---

is the Father, Holy the Son, Holy the Holy Spirit" (pp. 51, 86). The Egyptian or Alexandrian family on the other hand take up and expand the phrase: "Full are the heavens and the earth of Thy glory" (pp. 132, 176, 232).

[14] The Ambrosian Missal, which now has the Roman Canon, nevertheless to this day retains, in the Mass for Holy Saturday, a section commencing "Vere sanctus," awkwardly intercalated after the "Te igitur." But in at least two early MSS. of the Ambrosian rite, the "Vere sanctus" in the Mass of that day holds its original position as the sole connecting link between the Sanctus and the Qui pridie (Duchesne, *Origines du Culte,* pp. 205-6, and, with fuller details, Cagin, *Paleogr. Musicale,* v. 60 ff). And in the same MSS. there are relics, hardly less unmistakable, of the Gallican post Sanctus and post Pridie in the Mass for Maundy Thursday (Cagin, l.c.). The Stowe Missal has one clear instance (MacCarthy, p. 228) of a Gallican "Vere Sanctus"; besides which it has a similar section commencing "Benedictus qui venit" (p. 207), abbreviated, as MacCarthy shows, from a fuller "Vere Sanctus." This is so contrived as to lead up to "Te igitur"; which is obviously a conflate arrangement. Cagin, p. 69, mentions the first of these, but seems to have overlooked the second. He refers, however, to another Celtic fragment, discovered by H. B. Swete, similar to the first. On the Mozarabic and Gallican books see the following note.

[15] As the point does not seem to have been observed, precisely in this connection, before (though many of the instances have been given, for another purpose, by Cagin, pp. 58, 59), it may be well to give a list of the variants which I have noted. They occur in a considerable proportion of the 45 Masses which alone are available for comparison.
I. The Reichenau MS. (*P.L.* cxxxviii. 365 ff). Nos. 3 "Benedictus," &c.; 4, "Deus qui nos," &c.; 5, "Hic inquam Christus," &c.; 6, "Hanc in excelsis," &c.; 8, Unde terribilis, sanctus," &c.
II. "Missale Gothicum" (*P.L.* lxxii. 225 ff). Nos. 4, "Gloria," &c.; 20, "Suscipe,"

Whatever be the case, however, as regards the initial words of the original Roman "post Sanctus," it is, I think, safe to conclude that neither it nor the original Roman "post Pridie" (or Anamnesis plus Epiklesis) had a markedly intercessory character. The intercessory portion of the primitive liturgy would seem to have been exclusively pre-anaphoral. This, at any rate, is the impression produced by St. Justin's description and by the liturgy of the Church Ordinances. But, when once the unbroken continuity of the great Eucharistic prayer had been interrupted by the "Sanctus," an instinct which, because so universal, must be held to have been sound, would seem to have led to the introduction of intercessory prayers into the Anaphora itself.

And hence arose a kind of duplication which in a somewhat ponderous form is found to lengthen out unduly the Eastern liturgies. For in them the prayers described by St. Justin as put forth by the whole congregation, developed into the "Diakonika" or "Synapté" or "Ectené" which followed the Gospel; and the same ideas and petitions are expanded with hardly less prolixity in the great intercession which forms so large a portion of the Eastern Anaphora. But the Roman rite, in the course of its development, would seem to have skilfully

---

&c.; 27, "Haec est sine fine felicitas," &c.; 36, "Tuo jussu," &c.; 37, "Haec te nos," &c.; 49, "Hanc igitur," &c. (but this, of course, is Roman, and borrowed); 64, "Oremus dilectissimi," &c.; 65 and 80, "Hosanna," &c.; 78, "Sanctus in Sanctis," &c.; 79, "Per quem deprecemur," &c.

III. "Missale Gallicanum" *(ibid.* 339 ff). Nos. 1, "Benedictus plane," &c.; 4, "Hanc igitur" (Roman); 15, "Aspice," &c.; 17, "Te igitur" (Roman).

In view of these instances we must, I think, recognize the possibility that the form "Vere sanctus, vere benedictus," notwithstanding its constant occurrence in the Mozarabic Missal as revised by Card. Ximenes *(P.L.* lxxxv. 109 fif.) may, after all, be in the nature of a "survival of the fittest" among many competing forms. But this admission does not affect the argument from the general character of the Gallican post Sanctus, which (with the "Qui pridie") must surely have been derived, ultimately, from Rome.

Chapter XII: The Canon — III

avoided this ponderous duplication.[16] Nor is there, I think, any evidence at all to show that the intercessory portion of the Roman Canon was ever other than relatively short. And the substitution of "Te igitur," with its reference back to the body of the Preface, for the earlier "post Sanctus" with its subsumption of the Sanctus only, was as skilful a method as could have been devised for introducing the intercessory element into this central portion of the Mass, and at the same time preserving the essential continuity of the latter.

There is then, I believe, no serious reason for maintaining that the "Te igitur" and what follows it was transferred, whether textually or in substance, either from a position subsequent to the consecration, or, as I was formerly disposed to think, from the offertory. At the utmost it may with some approach to certainty be held that the Mementos, as prayers for particular persons, once had their place, in the Roman as in the early Gallican rite, before the preface. This however, is to be understood, of course, not of the verbal text of these prayers, but only of their general signification.

---

[16] That there is a certain duplication as between Offertory and Canon in the present Roman rite has been pointed out in vol. i. chap. vii. p. 109. But this is due to the intrusion of Gallican elements into the simpler Gregorian rite.

CHAPTER XIII
THE CANON - IV

T may perhaps seem strange, and hardly in accord with the sound principles of sound criticism (to use the word in its best and most legitimate sense), to have devoted so much space to the internal evidence, such as it is, supplied by the Canon itself as to the successive stages of its development, before even touching, except in the case of St. Justin's account of the liturgy, on the external testimony which bears, or may be thought to bear, on the subject. But for two reasons I have deliberately adopted this course. For, first, in this particular instance, the internal evidence appears to me to be, I dare not say clearer and more abundant, but at least less obscure and scanty than the external. And secondly, since the words of the Canon of the Mass form part, and in a sense incomparably the best part, of our daily vocal prayer, it seemed more profitable and helpful to concentrate the reader's attention on its structure and purport, rather than to distract his thoughts with the consideration of historical problems, which for him, perhaps, may have little of living interest.

The historical evidence cannot, however, be passed over in silence, and I proceed to summarize it as briefly as possible, looking backwards from what is clear and certain to the obscurity of the remoter past.

1. In the first place then it is certain that the Canon as we know it has come down to us unchanged from the days of St.

Gregory the Great.[1] On this point there is, of course, no room for dispute or discussion.

Secondly, it is for practical purposes certain that the changes introduced by St. Gregory into the Canon were, relatively speaking, small. They consisted, in fact, in the transfer of the "Pater noster" from its old position after the Fraction to that which it now holds,[2] and in the addition, or perhaps the fixing, of the formula "diesque nostros," &c., as the termination of the prayer "Hanc igitur." John the Deacon says that he "added" these words.[3] It would probably have been more correct to say that he substituted them for certain variant endings, such as are found, to the number of four or five, in the Leonianum, and such as probably occurred more frequently in the original text of the Gelasianum.[4]

3. Going back more than fifty years from St. Gregory, we have the clear and explicit testimony of Pope Vigilius (c. 540), writing to Bishop Profuturus of Braga, that in his time the text of the Roman Canon ("ipsius canonicae precis textus") was fixed, admitting only of minor variant clauses on particular festivals.[5]

4. Although we are not told that St. Gelasius (c. 490) made

---

[1] The addition of the "Agnus Dei" by Pope Sergius I (c. a.d. 700) lies, of course, outside the Canon. Nor is there any need to linger on certain interpolations in the Gregorian Canon which are found in many mediaeval MSS., but which were finally ruled out of court. Cf. Ebner, passim.

[2] See below, chap. xiv.

[3] *Vita Greg. Mag.* in *P.L.* lxxv. 94.

[4] All the variants in the extant MSS. of the Gelasianum conclude with the words "diesque nostros," &c. But this may probably be the result of that process of "Gregorianizing," which even the earliest of these MSS. have undergone.

[5] "Cognoscite ... nos semper eodem tenore oblata Dei munera consecrare." But on great festivals "singula capitula diebus apta subjungimus" (P.L. lxix. 18; cf. Fortescue, p. 135). These "capitula" would be of the same nature as the variant clauses in the "Communicantes" and "Hanc igitur" which have survived in our Missals, but more numerous.

Chapter XIII: The Canon — IV 143

any change in the Canon, yet the superscription "Canon dominicus Papae Gilasi," occurring in the Stowe Missal,[6] makes it necessary to take account of the possibility that he may be the author of any alteration in the order or wording of the prayers which can, on independent grounds, be proved to have been made about his time. Such would be, for instance, the elimination or modification of the epiklesis, now represented by the prayer "Supplices te rogamus," &c.[7] The superscription in question does not, of course, imply that the scribe believed Gelasius to have been the author of the Canon as a whole. At the utmost it implies a tradition that this Pope had in some way modified the text.

5. And in fact, when we go back to the earlier half of the fifth century we find what, by Dr. Fortescue and others, have been deemed to be clear indications that, if it was not effected by St. Gelasius himself, a notable re-arrangement of the parts of the Canon must have taken place in the interval. The writers referred to do not lay any undue stress on Pope Boniface's assurance (c. 420) to the Emperor Honorius that intercession is made for him "inter mysteria," *i.e.*, within the Canon or "Action" of the Mass.[8] But when Celestine I (c. 430), under similar circumstances, informs Theodosius that he is prayed for, by name, "oblatis sacrificiis," *i.e.*, "after the offering of the sacrifice,"[9] this testimony is regarded as all but conclusive in favor of the hypothesis that the "great intercession" formerly followed the consecration; and that its present "scattered" condition is due to the transfer of a portion of it to its present

---

[6] MacCarthy, p. 219.

[7] See above, p. 46.

[8] *Ep. ad Honorium*, P.L. xx. 767. "Ecce enim inter ipsa mysteria, inter preces suas quas pro vestra felicitate defundit imperii; ; cum sollicita petitione miscetur oratio ne nos ... semel evulsa distrahat a cultu solito ... discordia." It is just possible that these last words contain an allusion to the words "diesque nostros in tua pace," &c., of the "Hanc igitur."

[9] *Ep. ad Theodosium*, P.L. 1. 544.

place. Yet it may be doubted whether anyone would have thought of basing a serious argument on this expression were it not for a far more weighty piece of testimony which must presently be examined. Meanwhile I may express my own belief that Celestine's expression, "oblatis sacrificiis" are nothing but an echo of the words "haec sancta sacrificia illibata... quae tibi offerimus" (in the "Te igitur," where the Emperor's name was mentioned after that of Pope); and that they do not specifically refer to the consecration as such.

6. The more important testimony just referred to is of course the famous letter of Innocent I (c. 410) to Bishop Decentius of Gubbio. Gubbio is a city of Umbria, some twenty miles east of Perugia, and not so remote from Milan but that the bishop might be expected to know the Milanese practice, or even the Gallican, almost as well as he knew the Roman. He had written to the Pope to ask, among other things, whether the names "of those who had made offerings" (note the limitation) should be proclaimed before the Canon ("antequam precem sacerdos faciat"), or later. Innocent's answer, partly to the letter in general, and partly to this particular question, is to the following effect:

"If all bishops would observe in their integrity the apostolic traditions, there would be no diversities of ritual. But when everyone thinks himself at liberty to do what seems good in his own eyes without regard to tradition, such diversities inevitably arise, to the scandal of the faithful.

"What was delivered by St. Peter the prince of the Apostles to the Roman Church should be observed by all, nor should anything be added to or interpolated therein ('superduci aut introduci') except under authority, nor should any example be followed but that of Rome, from which the churches of Italy, Gaul, Spain, Africa and Sicily had their origin.

"As to the particular question concerning the proclamation of the names before the prex ('antequam precem sacerdos faciat'), and before the celebrant has by his prayer ('oratione') commended to God the gifts of those whose names are to be announced [which is precisely what is done in the "Te igitur"], you yourself will see how superfluous it is to bring in ('insinues') the name of him whose oblation you have not yet presented to God, as though He did not know it ('quamvis illi incognitum sit nihil'). First then the oblata are to be commended to God [as they are in the "Te igitur"], and then the names of those who have made the offerings are to be proclaimed ('edicenda'); so that they are to be named 'inter sacra mysteria' (*i.e.*, within the sacrificial action) and not in the course of what precedes it, that by the mysteries themselves we may open a way for the prayers that are to follow ('ut ipsis mysteris viam futuris precibus aperiamus')."[10]

Now if anyone will carefully examine this passage, and will compare it with the analysis of the Canon which has been given in Chapter x., or better still, with the text of the Canon itself, he can hardly fail to see how exactly the concluding paragraph, with the possible exception of the last clause of all, describes the actual position of the Memento for the living. It is by the "Te igitur," and not by any prayer that follows the consecration, that the oblata are "commended to God." After the consecration they have become God's gifts, which are no longer in any human sense ours. We could not, if we would, now withdraw them; they have ceased to be what the offerer originally presented. And the force of this consideration should make us hesitate to understand the last clause of all in any sense inconsistent with what has been said. Nor is it indeed necessary so to press "ipsa mysteria" ("the mysteries themselves") as if the phrase necessarily pointed specifically to the consecration. The whole of the action is designated by the term "mysteries," which could likewise be used, without impropriety, of that part of the action with which the writer of the letter has been concerned. Indeed, Innocent himself, in a later paragraph of the letter, reminds Decentius that on so

---

[10] *P.L.* xx. 552-554. It is to be remembered that the offertory prayers, now said by the priest after the Gospel, then had no place in the liturgy. See vol. i. chap. vii.

sacred and secret a theme, he must needs speak guardedly and obscurely. He writes: "Verba ... dicere non possum, ne magis prodere videar quam ad consultationem respondere," *i.e.*, he will not quote the very words of a sacramental prayer lest he should seem to be revealing secrets rather than answering a question.[11]

The allusion is of course to the "disciplina arcani," the "discipline of the secret," then in full force.[12]

But now, because some of my readers may after all be disposed to hold, with Dr. Fortescue, that there is a clear and unmistakable reference to the consecration in the Pope's words about "opening the way for prayers which are to follow by the mysteries themselves," it is important to notice that Innocent says nothing at all, either explicitly or by implication, about a "great intercession," and that both question and answer have to do, not with "names" in general (including, for instance, those of the Pope, the Bishop, and formerly the Emperor, occurring in the "Te igitur"), but exclusively about the names of the particular persons whose offerings entitled them to be prayed for. In other words, all that he says has reference to what, since the public recitation of names has been suppressed, we now call the "Memento for the living." And consequently, if his concluding expression is to be understood as implying that the "names" of which he speaks are to be read after the consecration, this will simply mean that in Innocent's time the Memento for the living immediately preceded the Memento for the dead. In any case (and this is the important point) he is not speaking of the "Te igitur" or "Communicantes" or of anything corresponding thereto.

In illustration of this statement it may be worth while to call attention to a passage in the seventh of the "Ordines Romani," which deals with the ritual of the Lenten "Scrutinies." It is here explicitly directed that, after the Gospel, an offering

---

[11] P.L. xx. 555. Cf. Probst, *Abendl. Messe*, p.148.

[12] Cf. vol. i. p. 52.

should be made by the parents or sponsors of the candidates for baptism, the "electi," as they are called, and then it is further directed that in the Memento for the living the names of the sponsors are to be recited, and those of the "electi" in the "Hanc igitur." Here, surely, is a clear illustration, all the better for being quite incidental, of what is meant by the "nomina offerentium" in Innocent's letter.[13]

Perhaps, then, enough has been said to convince the reader that the instructions given by Innocent I to Decentius of Gubbio afford no support whatever to the advocates of the hypothesis that the present condition of the Roman Canon is due to a subversive transference of the larger portion of an alleged "great intercession" from its supposedly original position after the consecration.

Of the very interesting quotation from the Canon of the Mass which is found in the Ambrosian tract "de Sacramentis," it must be enough to say that it bears witness to the existence, in the writer's time, of that portion of the Canon which extends from "Quam oblationem" to the end of the prayer, "Supra quae."[14] That the quoted passage shows sundry variants from the text as we know it, and that the two prayers "Unde et memores" and "Supra quae," following the consecration, are there fused into one, are facts which are familiar to all who have studied the subject. And the text would deserve to be closely examined here if we could be quite sure that the writer, in composing a catechetical tract, intended to reproduce his text with verbal exactness. But of this we cannot by any means be sure; and therefore I will content myself with emphasizing this point, that the "Quam oblationem," though it does not necessarily presuppose the "Hanc igitur," does presuppose the "Te igitur" or some equivalent form. From whence we may conclude that, in the all but contemporary days of Innocent I,

---

[13] *P.L.* lxxviii. 996.

[14] Of the date and probable authorship of this tract something has been said, above, in vol. i. p. 52.

the very chief among the prayers which the transpositionists would (on the strength of Innocent's letter) place after the consecration already had its present position. Nor can any stress be, I think, rightly laid on the circumstance that the writer says: "Sacerdos dicit: Fac nobis hanc oblationem ascriptam," &c.,[15] in other words, that he says "this" instead of "which." He could hardly quote, apart from its context, a passage beginning with a relative pronoun ("quam") without turning it into a demonstrative ("hanc").

Of earlier testimonies to the Canon there are none beyond the brief statements of the "Liber Pontificalis" about the "Sanctus" and the "Qui pridie," which have been already mentioned.

---

[15] *P.L.* xvi. 443.

CHAPTER XIV
THE PATER NOSTER, THE FRACTION, AND THE COMMUNION

O ONE, perhaps, who has assisted with attention at High Mass, can have failed to be struck with the analogy between the chant of the preface, which leads up to the "Sanctus," and that of the "praefatiuncula" or "little preface" ("Praeceptis salutaribus moniti," &c.), by which the Pater Noster is introduced. And the similarity must have been much more striking when the Pater Noster, as well as the Sanctus, was chanted or recited aloud by the whole congregation. The old Gallican liturgy carries the analogy a step further. For just as the Gallican post Sanctus, as has been seen, takes up and develops the leading words and ideas of the Sanctus and Benedictus, so the "Libera nos," or Embolism as it is called, takes up and develops the last petition of the Lord's Prayer. In the Roman rite the greater preface alone is variable, and this within strict limits, while the little preface and the embolism are fixed formulae, and the post Sanctus has disappeared in favor of the "Te igitur." The Gallican rite on the other hand exhibits the following complete parallelism:

Preface (variable).
SANCTUS.
Post Sanctus (variable).
Praefatiuncula (variable).
PATER NOSTER.
Embolism (variable).

It may be of interest to give a single example of a Gallican praefatiuncula and embolism respectively. They are from different Masses. The first of these prayers is indeed of such singular excellence as a piece of ecclesiastical Latin, in regard of the balance of phrases and the terseness of expression, that it seems worth while to give, in parentheses, the Latin corresponding to the very inadequate English translation.

Praefatiuncula. "Acknowledge, O Lord, the words which Thou hast prescribed, pardon the presumption which Thou hast commanded ('Agnosce, Domine, verba quae praecepisti, ignosce praesumptioni quam imperasti'). For it were ignorance not to know the grounds of our trust ('Ignorantia est enim non posse meritum,' *i.e.,* not to recognize that the merits in virtue of which we make our petition are not ours, but those of Christ our Lord), and it were contumacious not to obey the precept ('contumacia non servare praeceptum') whereby we are bidden to say: Our Father," &C.[1]

Embolism. "Deliver us from evil, O God, Author of all good; deliver us from every temptation, from every scandal, from every heresy, from all the works of darkness; establish us in every good work, and grant peace in our days, O God, Author of peace and of truth."[2]

Of the remarkable and significant affinity of the Gallican praefatiunculae and embolisms, notwithstanding their variability, with the corresponding invariable formulae in the Roman, something will have to be said in Chapter xvi. Meanwhile it is to be observed that, whereas the Eastern liturgies place the solemn Fraction of the Host after the Pater Noster, in the Gallican and Mozarabic rites this ceremony precedes the Lord's prayer, and we have the clear though somewhat indirect testimony of St. Gregory the Great that such, down to his own time, was the custom in the Roman Church also. Indeed it can hardly be doubted that the change

---

[1] *P.L.* lxxii. 317; Neale and Forbes, *Gallican Liturgies,* p. 150.

[2] *P.L.* ibid. 314; Neale and Forbes, p. 146. Cf. Lucas in *Dublin Revie-w,* Jan. 1894, p. 114.

Chapter XIV: The Pater Noster, Fraction, and Communion

introduced by St. Gregory was suggested by the eastern usage. It has been objected against Gregory, by John of Syracuse, that he had introduced Byzantine customs into the Roman liturgy, and in particular "that you have ordered the Lord's prayer to be recited immediately after the Canon" (*i.e.*, before and not after the fraction). In reply the Pope gives as his reason that "it seems very incongruous (valde inconveniens) that we should recite over the sacrifice (super oblationem) a prayer which was compiled by a liturgiologist (precem quam scholasticus composuerat) and that we should not say, over the Body and Blood of our Redeemer, the prayer which He Himself delivered to us."[3]

So far all is plain. But it unfortunately happens that the words which in St. Gregory's letter immediately precede those which have just been quoted, have been strangely misconstrued even down to our own days; and as the question as to their meaning is of some importance for the right understanding of the history of the liturgy, it may be worth while to examine them somewhat closely. The sentence rims as follows:—

"Orationem vero dominicam mox post precem dicimus quia mos apostolorum fuit ut ad ipsam solummodo orationem oblationis hostiam consecrarent."

Now the meaning of the first clause in this sentence ("We recite the Lord's prayer immediately after the prex") is plain enough; but the rendering of the second clause ("quia mos apostolorum fuit," &c., *i.e.*, "because it was the custom of the Apostles," &c.) has been keenly disputed. What was it that the Apostles were accustomed to do? What was the "mos apostolorum" here indicated? The answer to this question depends on the further question whether we are to construe together the words "oblationis hostiam" ("the sacrificial host,"—literally "the host of offering"), or "orationem oblationis" ("the sacrificial prayer"—literally "the prayer of offering"). As a matter of mere latinity, apart from all regard to

---

[3] *Epist.* ix. 12 (*P.L.* lxxviii. 955 ff.).

liturgical phraseology, the first rendering might seem preferable, as indeed it has seemed preferable to almost innumerable writers on the subject. But then, if this were the right construction, we should have to believe that St. Gregory believed what is, I think, quite incredible, viz., that the Apostles "were accustomed to consecrate the sacrificial host with no other accompaniment than the prayer," *i.e.*, the Our Father! Now, following Probst, I am convinced that St. Gregory's meaning is very far removed from this. Indeed, one might almost say that it is the very reverse of this. Join the words "orationem oblationis" and see what the sense is then. "The Apostles," we now read, "were accustomed to consecrate the host with no other accompaniment than the sacrificial prayer." Now "the sacrificial prayer" is, of course, the "prex," that is to say, the Canon, plus the preface. In other words, the Lord's Prayer had no place in the central portion ("the sacrificial prayer") of the primitive liturgy. This is straightforward and intelligible, and is, moreover, entirely credible. And it is not only credible, but, I believe, almost demonstrably true. The Lord's Prayer has, in fact, no place in the anaphora of the liturgy, either of the Apostolic Constitutions, or of the Ethiopic Church Ordinances, or of Serapion.[4] Moreover, whereas the phrase "oblationis hostia" is, so far as syntax goes, good Latin, it is, so far as meaning is concerned, distinctly tautological; for what kind of a "host" could there be which was not "sacrificial" or not "offered"? On the other hand "oratio oblationis" ("the sacrificial prayer" or "prayer of offering") is a technical term which precisely and literally represents the Greek εὐχὴ προσφορᾶς. "Oratio oblationis" is, in fact. Funk's rendering of εὐχὴ προσφόρου (sic) where it occurs as a quite distinctive superscription to the preface of Serapion's liturgy.[5] This document was not published till many years after Probst had first urged that we should construe "orationem oblationis" and

---

[4] Funk, *Didascalia*, i. 515; ii. 101, 177.

[5] Funk, *Didascalia*, ii. 172.

not "oblationis hostiam"; and it affords a somewhat remarkable confirmation of a theory which now deserves, as it seems to me, to be regarded as satisfactorily established.[6]

The only serious difficulty, or apparently serious difficulty, which militates against the acceptance of this conclusion lies in the little word "quia." It seems odd, at first sight, that St. Gregory should say that he has done something "because" the Apostles did otherwise. But his "because" must be taken as affecting not merely the words which immediately follow, but the whole of the succeeding context. The sense is "I have done this because whereas the Apostles used only the 'prayer of oblation' it seemed to me incongruous," and the rest.

In its present position the Pater noster marks the transition from the strictly sacrificial to what has been called the sacramental portion of the Mass. For while, on the one hand, it is plain that St. Gregory the Great desired to bring this prayer into close relation with the body of the Canon, on the other hand the petition, "Give us this day our daily bread," was unquestionably referred, from the earliest times, to that heavenly food the sacramental reception whereof is essential to the fullest participation in the fruits of the Holy Sacrifice.

The sequence of ideas in the prayers and rites which immediately follow the Pater noster is worthy of attention. The "Libera nos" which (as has been seen) takes up and develops the concluding words of the Lord's Prayer, ends with a petition for peace; the fraction is immediately followed by the versicle "Pax Domini sit semper vobiscum" with its response; the "Agnus Dei" concludes with the petition "Dona nobis pacem," and it is followed by yet another prayer for peace ("O Lord Jesus Christ, who didst say to Thine Apostles: Peace I leave you," &c.), which in its turn serves to introduce the "Kiss of Peace" in its present modified form. It is plain enough that

---

[6] Probst, *Liturgie der drei esten Jahrhunderten* (1870), pp. 355 f. Cf. J. R. Gasquet in *Dublin Review,* April 1890, p. 286; Lucas in *Dublin Review,* Jan. 1894, p. 112 note.

there has been development and expansion at this point in the liturgy, though the steps of the development are not easy to trace.[7] Some of them, however, will be incidentally indicated in what follows.

In the first place it must be noted that the fraction of the Host originally had a definite purpose which has become entirely obscured in the course of liturgical history. The primitive altar-breads were very much larger than those which are now in use; and when the Host was broken, this was done, after the pattern set by our Lord Himself, in order that the assistant clergy might receive Communion in the form of particles therefrom. Another particle was reserved, to be consumed by the celebrant at a future Mass, in token of the essential one-ness of the Holy Sacrifice, whenever and wherever it might be offered. And the same truth was emphasized by another custom which, in Rome at least, prevailed during several centuries. This was the custom of sending, by the hands of duly ordained acolytes, to whom this precious privilege belonged, consecrated particles from the Host of the Pope's Mass, to such bishops as might be staying in the city and celebrating at the same time as the Pope himself. Indeed, the familiar phrase, "in communion with the Holy See," may not improbably have had its origin in this usage, or was at least closely connected therewith.[8] Before leaving the subject of the "fermentum," however, for such was the name by which these consecrated particles were designated, it will be worth while to quote, in a slightly abridged form, Dr. Fortescue's interesting passage on the subject:—

"From about the fourth century down to about the tenth we hear constantly that Popes and other bishops sent something called 'fermentum' to their priests. Anastasius Bibliothecarius,

---

[7] Cf. Fortescue, p. 371.

[8] The last three paragraphs are borrowed from the author's "Notes on the Mass" in *The Xaverian*, 1909. But Dr. Fortescue has dealt with this subject much more fully, as will be seen.

Chapter XIV: The Pater Noster, Fraction, and Communion

writing in the ninth century, says that Pope Melchiades (311–314) 'ordered that oblations for the consecration by the bishop should be sent to the churches, which is called the 'fermentum.'[9] ... We have a contemporary reference in the letter of Innocent I (401–417) to Decentius, already quoted. He says that the 'fermentum' is taken by acolytes on Sunday 'per titulos' (that is to the titular Roman churches), so that priests who on that day cannot concelebrate or communicate at the Pope's altar may know that they are not 'separated from our communion.' But he does not wish it to be taken 'per paroecias' (the country parishes?) nor to secondary churches (outside the city) 'because the sacraments are not to be carried a long way.'[10] ... It is clear that the 'fermentum' was the Holy Eucharist. Innocent's words about 'carrying the sacraments' are plain; in Ordo Rom. I we find the bishop (not Pope) using the 'particula fermenti quod ab Apostolico consecratum est' [i.e., the particle consecrated by the Pope] just as the Pope uses the 'Sancta' [the particle consecrated at a previous Mass] mixing it with the consecrated wine at the Pax.[11] The use and idea of the 'fermentum' then are obvious. It corresponds to the 'Sancta.' The Pope sent a fragment of the host consecrated by him to the suburban bishops [? or bishops present in Rome] and Roman parish priests. As the 'Sancta' was a symbol of the identity of the sacrifice from one Mass to another, so was the 'fermentum' a sign of union between the bishop and his clergy. As far back as Victor I (190–202) we find the same custom. St. Irenaeus reminds him that he sends the Eucharist to other bishops.[12] One cannot conceive a more pregnant symbol of unity and intercommunion. ...It may be noted that the meaning of the word is

---

[9] *P.L.* cxxvii. 1499 f.; *Lib. Pont.* (Duchesne) i. 168 f. (Fortescue's notes are here abridged.

[10] *P.L.* xx. 556 f.; Bona I. xxiii. 8.

[11] *P.L.* lxxviii. 948.

[12] Eusebius, *Hist. Eccl.*, v. 24.

primarily symbolic. 'Fermentum' is not quite the same as 'fermentatum.' The idea seems to have been [nay, most certainly was] that this particle of the Holy Eucharist [or rather, the Holy Eucharist itself] unites the Church as leaven unites bread."[13]

In the above passage I have omitted sentences dealing with the real or supposed difficulty as to the use of leavened or unleavened bread. I doubt whether any argument, under this head, can be drawn from the use of the word "fermentum." The term is (as Dr. Fortescue says) "primarily symbolic." The Holy Eucharist was in very truth the principal means whereby the Church was not merely "united" but "leavened." It only remains to say that, when the practices above described fell into disuse they left us only a shrunken survival in "the commixture of a particle of the host just consecrated."[14] This "intinction" or "embolism" has, however, a significance of its own, and though a survival is yet no mere survival. It is commonly and, as it would seem, correctly held to be symbolical of the re-union of the Body and Blood of our Lord when He resumed His human life—under new conditions—at the Resurrection. From all that has been said it plainly appears that the fraction was, in its origin, much more obviously than it is at present, an act immediately preparatory to Holy Communion.[15]

The "Agnus Dei," as we know it, was introduced into the liturgy, at this point, by Pope Sergius I (c. 700).[16] It would seem to have been originally a choral chant only, the words not being recited by the celebrant, but sung while he prayed in secret. It

---

[13] Fortescue, pp. 368 ff.

[14] P. 369.

[15] Of the elaborate symbolical fractions which characterize the Eastern, Mozarabic, and Celtic rites space will not allow me to speak here.

[16] So the Lib. Pont. (Duchesne i. 376 apud Fortescue, p. 387). Its presence in MSS. of the Gregorianum is probably due to interpolation. I say, above, "at this point," because, in a slightly different form, the "Agnus Dei" is already found in the "Gloria in Excelsis."

is beyond doubt that, at first, each invocation concluded with the words "Miserere nobis," a usage which still survives in the one single Church of St. John Lateran. "During the Middle Ages on Maundy Thursday the Agnus Dei was sung with 'Miserere nobis' thrice. Gihr accounts for this as a result of the omission of the kiss of peace on that day.[17] It can be explained more naturally by the fact that the station is at St. John Lateran."[18] It is not an improbable conjecture that the substitution of the petition, "Dona nobis pacem," in the third invocation, had for its purpose to bring the "Agnus Dei," into closer harmony with the dominant idea of "peace," which, as has been seen, pervades this portion of the Mass. Yet, even now, there is, be it said with all reverence, a certain anomaly in the separation of the salutation "Pax Domini sit semper vobiscum," which immediately follows the fraction, from the actual giving of the kiss of peace.

With reference to the Pax itself, it is to be observed that its position in the Roman Mass is all but unique. In every one of the Eastern liturgies, as also in the early Gallican and Mozarabic rites, and almost certainly in the earlier Ambrosian, the kiss of peace is or was given, not before the Communion, but at the commencement of the sacrificial portion of the Mass, *i.e.*, immediately or all but immediately after the dismissal of the catechumens and penitents. And it is safe to infer that this must have been its original place in the Roman liturgy also.[19] The only possible objection to this conclusion may be found in some words of Tertullian's tract "on Prayer," which have been thought to indicate that, in the African rite of the second and

---

[17] Gihr, *Das h. Messopfer*, p. 671, n. 2.

[18] Fortescue, pp. 387 f.

[19] St. Justin's testimony would be unexceptionable if we could be quite sure that he is describing the Roman practice, and not, as seems to me more probable, that of Ephesus (see above, chap. ix.). "Ἀλλήλους φιλήματι ἀσπασόμεθα παυσάμενοι τῶν εὐχῶν. "Επειτα προσφέρεται ... ἄρτος καὶ ποτήριον κτλ. (Apol. i., 65).

third centuries, the Pax occurred (as in our own rite) after the Pater noster. "Africa," says Dr. Fortescue, herein agreeing with Dom F. Cabrol, "was certainly similar to Rome in its liturgy, and Africa had the Kiss of Peace very much where we have it now, in connection with the Lord's Prayer, just before the Communion."[20] But this statement appears to me little short of misleading. The contention that Tertullian's words about the kiss of peace have any reference to the Pater noster as recited in the Mass, is, to say the least, by no means convincing. For the writer has already passed, in a previous chapter, from the consideration of the Lord's prayer in particular to that of prayer—or public prayer—in general.[21] "Dom Cabrol notes," says Dr. Fortescue elsewhere, "that the 'Kiss of Peace' was the ceremony which accompanied all public prayers (de Orat. xviii.)." But a passage which deals with "a ceremony which accompanied all public prayers" cannot legitimately be cited as an authority for the precise position which that ceremony held in the liturgy of the Mass.[22]

Nor is the reason or motive which may probably have led

---

[20] Fortescue, p. 370, referring to Tertullian *"de Orat.* 10,14,18 (*P.L.* i. 1281)", which should be, as given on p. 41, de Orat. 18 (P.L. i. 1176 f.), and to St. Augustine, *"Sermo*vi. (*P.L.* xxxviii. 561,565)", where there is clearly an error, for neither in Serm. vi. (col. 59 ff.) nor on col. 561, 565 (*Serm.* xc.) is there anything bearing on the subject. Perhaps the reference should be to *Serm.* ccxxvii. *(P.L.* xxxviii. 1101), where the position of the Pax between the Pater Noster and the Communion is quite explicitly indicated. But "it would not, perhaps, be safe to rely on this testimony, for the sermon is by some ascribed to St. Caesarius of Arles, who lived more than a century later" than St. Augustine (Lucas in *Dublin Review, l.c.* p. 128; cf. Venables in *Diet. Chr. Antiq.*, p. 904), and in any case the witness of St. Augustine is not available for the second or third century. He was contemporary with Innocent I, in whose time the supposedly altered Roman practice may be supposed to have taken root in Africa, even if it did not originate thence.

[21] "Praemissa legitima et ordinaria oratione *(i.e.* the Pater Noster) quasi fundamento, *accidentium jus est desideriorum, jus est superfluendi extrinsecus petitiones,* cum memoria tamen praeceptorum," &c. (c. x. *P.L.* i. 1165).

[22] But cf. Cabrol, *Diet. dArch. Chr.* i. 604.

Chapter XIV: The Pater Noster, Fraction, and Communion

to the transfer of the Pax to its present position far to seek, though I know of no writer who has explicitly called attention to it. It is, however, plainly suggested by Mr. Jenner when he says: "The Roman rite, which has completely obliterated all distinction between the 'Missa Catechumenorum' and the 'Missa Fidelium' associates this sign of unity, not with the beginning of the latter but with the Communion, and this position is as old as the letter of St. Innocent I (416) to Decentius of Gubbio."[23] It is at least possible that the "obliteration" of which Mr. Jenner here speaks was intentional, at least after what might nowadays be called a "subconscious" fashion. At any rate, whether consciously intentional or not, it involved, probably in successive stages, a triple transfer, viz., (1) of the chief collect to its present position in the Roman Mass; (2) of the "Nomina," with their accompanying prayers, to the Canon; and (3) of the Pax. When the dismissal of the catechumens had ceased to form part of the daily or weekly ceremonial, the point in the liturgy at which it had previously taken place ceased to have that special significance, or to deserve that prominence, which it had once possessed; and just as the beginning of the whole service now seemed the most suitable position of the chief collect, so also no more appropriate position could have been found for the Pax than that which it now holds just before the Communion. It is, however, on its appropriateness as setting the seal of ratification on all that has been done, that St. Innocent lays stress in the letter to Decentius, and he seems to imply that the present position of the Pax was not the result of some recent innovation, but was already of long standing.[24]

---

[23] *Catholic Encyclopedia*, vi. 362 (11). Italics mine. For "as old as," in the above passage, it would have been better to write "older than" the letter of St. Innocent.

[24] His words are: "Cum post omnia quae aperire non debeo pax sit necessario indicenda, per quam constet populum ad omnia quae in mysteriis aguntur ... praebuisse consensum, ac finita esse pacis concludentis signaculo

The "Domine, non sum dignus," affords, like the "Agnus Dei," an excellent example of the apt application of a text from the Gospel to a sublime mystery with which, in its original context, it had no relation; except indeed that relation of all-pervading analogy which binds together into one living whole, the incidents of our Lord's life on earth, and the sacramental system by means of which His ceaseless beneficence is continued through the ages.

Dr. Fortescue has an interesting passage, here reproduced in substance, in which he suggests that "the little group of prayers at the Communion of the people" were (probably) borrowed from the ceremony of private administration of the Holy Sacrament. This ceremony is itself a sort of brief compendium of certain portions of the Mass. It begins with the "Asperges," in a form reminiscent of the introit; the Confiteor follows and is itself followed by a collect; after which "Ecce Agnus Dei" echoes, says Dr. Fortescue, the "Agnus Dei" of the Mass, from which also the "Domine non sum dignus" is obviously borrowed. And these items, originally taken over from the Mass, are here reintroduced into the liturgy.[25]

The somewhat fragmentary invocation which in a modem missal is called "Communio"—affords an opportunity for saying a few words about the choral portions of the Mass. These choral pieces may be roughly divided into three classes, viz., responses, hymns and antiphons. The responses call for no special remark. The word "hymn" in the above classification must be taken in a wide sense, as including not only the "sequences" which on certain occasions follow the gradual (i.e., the "Victimae Paschali" at Easter, the "Veni Sancte Spiritus" at Whitsuntide, the "Lauda Sion" on Corpus Christi, the "Stabat Mater" and the "Dies Irae"), but also the Kyrie Eleison, the Gloria in Excelsis, the Credo, the Sanctus and Benedictus, and the Agnus Dei. Of these, some, like the Gloria in Excelsis, the

---

demonstrentur" (P.L. xx. 553).

[25] Fortescue,pp. 384f., citingKrazer,De... antiquisEccl. occid. liturgiis(1786).

sequence and the Credo interrupt the course of the service as performed by the celebrant at the altar, the sacred ministers sitting down till the conclusion of the chant. Others, like the Sanctus and the Benedictus, are sung while the celebrant continues to recite those prayers which (for this very reason) are to be said "secreto—in a whisper," or, like the Domine non sum dignus, "moderata voce," *i.e.*, loud enough to be heard by the attendants, but not so as to interrupt the singing. But in two respects the antiphons, and in particular the introit, the offertory, and the communion differ from the hymns. In the first place they are taken, normally at least, from the psalms. Indeed, each of them may be regarded as the shrunken survival of a complete psalm with its doxology and antiphon. And secondly they were originally intended to fill up certain intervals during which something was being done which otherwise would have been done in silence. Thus the introit, as has been seen, was sung while the celebrant entered the church and proceeded to the altar; the offertory while the oblata were presented and received; the "Communio," as its name denotes, while the faithful received the Holy Sacrament.

Bona affirms that at least on some occasions the antiphon of the offertory psalm was repeated as a refrain after each verse or two, like the invitatory at Matins; but the point is one which I must be content to leave to those who have made a study of the history of the ecclesiastical chant.[26] The survival of the antiphon alone, in the case of the offertory, seems to point to a time when the only prayer recited at the oblation of the unconsecrated host and chalice was the secreta, with its invitatory introduction, "Orate fratres," and the response thereto. The fact that the invitation and response are to be said "moderata voce," and the prayer itself recited, as its name denotes, "secreto," may be taken as a clear indication that the

---

[26] "Apud Gregorium singula offertoria plures versus habent, adjunctos, et quandoque integer psalmus repetita post singulos versus antiphona cantari solebat" (Bona, n. viii. 3).

choir were, so to say, "in possession." Nor is it to be supposed that, down to comparatively modern times, mottets *ad libitum* were sung during this portion of the Mass.

The gradual and the Alleluia antiphon (or the tract which replaces the latter in ferial Masses) stand on a somewhat different footing. They were, originally, not merely chants intended to fill up an interval during which something was being done, but instances of the very ancient liturgical principle according to which scripture lessons were made to alternate with psalmody, as in the Matins of the Breviary. The origin and significance of the name "Gradual" has been explained in Chapter VI.

It has already been observed, but the statement will bear repetition here, that the postcommunion prayer, at least in the older Masses, for the most part explicitly assumes that all the faithful who are present have received Holy Communion. This prayer is in fact the public and official "thanksgiving" of the entire congregation, immediately after which the faithful were dismissed with the words "Ite, missa est"; words from which, as has been said, the Mass (missa, *i.e.*, missio, dismissal) takes its name.

CHAPTER XV
THE SAINTS AND THE MASS

THAT the Mass, being a sacrifice, and indeed the supreme sacrifice, cannot be offered to our Lady or to any saint, every Catholic child who has been even moderately well instructed is perfectly aware.

But it is very possible that some of our readers may never have noticed that the Mass contains not so much as a single prayer addressed to the Blessed Virgin or to any of the saints. All the prayers of the Mass, without exception, are addressed to God Himself, as befits petitions which pertain to a distinctively sacrificial ritual. The only apparent exception to the foregoing statement is to be found in certain invocations which very occasionally occur, or may occur, in the choral portion of the Mass, as, for instance, in the "Stabat Mater," which forms the "sequence" of the Mass on the Feast of the Seven Dolours of Our Lady.

Nevertheless, our Lady and the saints, though not directly invoked in the prayers of the Eucharistic liturgy, hold a highly-honoured place in relation to the Mass; and this to an extent which may possibly surprise those who have not closely attended to the matter.

In the first place it is most strictly enjoined by the laws of the Church that beneath every altar on which the Holy Sacrifice is offered, or in a cavity of the table of the altar itself, some relics of martyrs should be enshrined. This usage goes back, of course, to the days when Mass was offered, in the catacombs, on the very tombs of those who had sealed their confession of the Christian faith by a martyr's death. But it has, moreover, a scriptural basis and justification in the words of the

Apocalypse: "I saw under the altar the souls of them that were slain for the Word of God and for the testimony which they held."[1] And it is full of a most profound and beautiful and encouraging significance. For it reminds us that all the sufferings of the martyrs, and indeed all the sufferings for justice's sake even of those faithful servants of God who are not in the strict sense martyrs, are fused, as it were, and made one with the sufferings of Christ our Lord, being accepted by God as an efficacious sacrifice; efficacious precisely by virtue of their union with His self-offering.

Secondly, every Mass assigned to a saint's day has a collect, secreta and postcommunion in which God's mercy is asked "through the intercession" of the servant of God whose feast is being kept.

But thirdly, in addition to this, those fixed and unchanging prayers which are common to all Masses contain repeated references to the saints, as follows:

(a) In the "Confiteor" we call, as witnesses of our acknowledgment of sin, and as intercessors for pardon, the Blessed Virgin Mary, St. Michael as representing the heavenly hosts, St. John the Baptist, as representative of the saints of the Old Testament, SS. Peter and Paul as representing those of the New, and finally "all the saints" without exception. It is, assuredly, a distinguished audience to which we make our appeal; and it would be the height of bad manners if, in the very act of inviting such an audience to listen to us, we were ourselves to pay little attention to what we are saying, or again (as sometimes happens) to mumble the words of our invitation.

(b) On ascending to the predella after the Confiteor, the celebrant kisses the altar begging the intercession of the martyrs whose relics are enclosed therein *"quorum reliquiae hic sunt"*—and "of all the saints."

(c) After the Lavabo, in the prayer, "Suscipe Sancta Trinitas," the elements, as yet unconsecrated, are offered in

---

[1] Apoc. 6:9.

Chapter XV: The Saints and the Mass 165

memory of the passion, resurrection and ascension of our Lord, and in honour of our Lady, St. John the Baptist, SS. Peter and Paul, those whose relics are contained in or beneath the altar, and "of all the saints"; and their intercession is asked.

(d) In the Canon, at the "Communicantes," commemoration is made of our Lady, of the Apostles (including St. Paul, but not St. Mathias), and of twelve martyrs, five of them Popes, and all of them except St. Cyprian connected with Rome. The number, twelve, must be taken of course as indicating that those who are enumerated are named as representing the rest; though here, as elsewhere, explicit mention is likewise made of "all the saints." In many early liturgical manuscripts, as, *e.g.*, in the Stowe Missal, the list is expanded so as to include the names of local saints; and it may be mentioned here that the earliest form of "canonization" consisted in the placing of a name in this position of honour. No one, however, will nowadays question the wisdom of restricting the enumeration of names to a manageable number; and no selection could be more aptly representative than that of those whom the local Roman Church delighted to honour. For it must not be forgotten that the Missal, as has been said in a previous chapter, is a distinctively Roman book—originally the Pope's own Mass-book—the use of which was at first gradually adopted, and at last authoritatively prescribed, throughout Western Christendom.

(e) In the "Nobis quoque peccatoribus" we ask that we may be found not unworthy to have a part "with the holy Apostles and martyrs," after which words another characteristic and representative enumeration occurs. The Apostles, indeed, are not individually named, but after "St. John," *i.e.*, the Baptist, the last of the Old Testament saints and himself a glorious martyr, there occur the names, deliberately selected, of seven men and seven women, all of them martyrs for the faith, with, as usual, a concluding mention of "all the saints."

So far I had written in 1909. To Dr. Fortescue's learned

pages I am indebted for some further remarks on the list of saints contained in the "Nobis quoque," which are worth quoting here, as emphasizing, among other points, the carefully calculated and strictly supplementary character of this list.

"In all rites the celebrant prays for the living and the dead and remembers the Saints. But the order in which these three elements of the Intercession follow one another varies.... The names of the Saints here are arranged in a scheme, as at the 'Communicantes.' First comes St. John (as our Lady in the other list), then seven men and seven women. There is evidently an intention of not repeating the names already mentioned, but of supplementing the former list, to which 'cum tuis sanctis apostolis et martyribus' seems to contain a general allusion.[2] Who is the John here named? ... It must be the Baptist. St. John the Evangelist had already been named in the 'Communicantes,' other lists repeat no names, not even our Lady's.... St. Stephen follows as the first martyr, again an unaccountable (?) omission in the former list, and St. Matthias and St. Barnabas, left out from the Apostles before. Ignatius of Antioch, Pope Alexander I (109—119), Marcellinus, a priest, and Peter, an exorcist martyred at Silva Candida under Diocletian, make up the list of men. The women are all well known. All Saints here are Martyrs, all are either Roman or saints popular at Rome."[3]

In the above passage Dr. Fortescue has deserved well of all students of the Roman liturgy. But I do not know why, in a sentence which has not been quoted, the omission of St. John the Baptist from the first list should be called "an obvious fault," or that of St. Stephen "unaccountable." The saints enumerated in "Communicantes" are "apostles and martyrs," the martyrs enumerated are Roman or (as St. Cyprian) closely connected with Rome. St. John the Baptist was not an apostle and St. Stephen was not a Roman martyr. They accordingly find

---

[2] A slight verbal transposition has been ventured on, here.

[3] Fortescue, pp. 356 f.

their place, and a very distinguished place, in the second enumeration.

(f) Finally, in the "Libera nos," we beg that our Lady, SS. Peter and Paul and St. Andrew "and all the Saints" may by their intercession, obtain for us the boon of peace. Here again the enumeration is manifestly "representative." It is indeed not easy to feel sure as to the reason for the mention of St. Andrew here. Possibly no other is needed than that he was St. Peter's brother, and that as such he is named with him.

It would, in the present writer's opinion, be altogether futile to seek any recondite explanation of the number and the present distribution of these six references to the intercession of our brethren in heaven. It may be sufficient to recognize that a wise Providence controls, to beneficent ends, even what might seem to us to be purely accidental. And we may well be thankful that, as things are, the memory of the saints, and our need of their intercession, is so repeatedly brought to mind in the liturgy of the Mass. "Our conversation is in Heaven," says St. Paul, who elsewhere reminds us of the "crowd of witnesses" who, from the heights of Heaven, witness all our struggles here below; and daily at the commencement of the most solemn portion of the Mass, the Church bids us to "lift up our hearts" to heavenly things. This is precisely what the frequent mention of the saints, our brethren, our exemplars, our witnesses, our intercessors, will help us to do, if only we take the trouble to attend to the words which we use, or which the celebrant utters on our behalf, during Holy Mass.

CHAPTER XVI
THE ROMAN AND THE EARLY GALLICAN RITES

THE statement has been made more than once in the course of this work that the liturgies of the Western Church had a common origin, and that this origin was distinctively Roman. It was "Eastern" only in the sense in which Christianity itself came from the East, and certainly not in the sense that, apart from incidental and sporadic borrowings, any one of the Western liturgies can be traced, or with any possibility referred, to any but a Roman source. This is a statement which ought, I venture to think, to have been long since regarded as beyond dispute. But because the origin of the Gallican rite, with which the Ambrosian and the Mozarabic are confessedly closely allied, has quite recently been once more declared to be a problem that awaits solution, it may be worth while to restate, here, the reasons which, more than twenty years ago, led the present writer to the conclusion that the "problem" even then admitted of a simple and satisfactory solution.

To state the solution first, leaving the reasons which support it to be subsequently set forth, it is to this effect. The structural differences which distinguish the early Gallican rite from the Roman liturgy as we know it are to be accounted for by the not unreasonable hypothesis that, in the course of three or four centuries, both rites had undergone considerable modifications and developments since the days when the remoter churches, at their foundation, brought their liturgy with them from Rome. The course of development in Rome itself proceeded by way of successive and gradual changes made by authority. The changes thus made in Rome were by no means all adopted in Lombardy, Gaul and Spain; others, adopted in principle, were in these countries carried to extremes,—a point on which something further will be said in the concluding paragraphs of this chapter.

The only point in which the conclusion here formulated differs from that which was put forward in certain publications to be presently quoted, is this. In former years I had too easily assumed that, at some time in the course of the fourth century, probably in the time of St. Damasus, the Roman liturgy had undergone "a drastic reform," in which the Gallican and Spanish churches had not shared. But for such a drastic reform there is no evidence; and by the one far-reaching change, viz., the substitution of variable for unvarying prayers and formulas, which, either in the fourth century, or possibly even in the third, undoubtedly was made in the Roman rite, the Gallican and Spanish Churches, and those of Lombardy too, were not only affected but, for lack of salutary restraint, affected quite unduly.

Apart from sundry differences of opinion on minor points, the main proposition as to the Roman origin of the early Gallican liturgy, and as to the general causes of the differences which distinguish it from the Roman rite in the earliest form in which the latter comes before us as an organized whole, was first put forward by Probst (in his *Liturgie der drei ersten Jahrhunderten*) in 1870, as also in his later works; then, with the support of fresh evidence to be hereafter given, by the present writer in a couple of articles contributed to The Dublin Review, in 1893—4; and two years later by Dom P. Cagin, in a very learned dissertation published in the fifth volume of the Paleographie Musicale (1896).[1] Father Cagin's view is

---

[1] "In a long Introduction to the Ambrosian Antiphonary, which he has published in *facsimile* from a MS. in the British Museum, [Father Cagin] takes occasion to enquire into the relation of the early Gallican to the early Roman liturgy. It is plain that he has not seen the *Dublin* articles, and it is all the more gratifying to find that he not only agrees with the main conclusions arrived at by the writer [of them], but bases [these conclusions]

Chapter XVI: The Roman and Early Gallican Rite 171

supported, in the main, by Dom F. Cabrol in *Les Origines Liturgiques* (1906), and is, I believe, maintained by more than one of the contributors to the *Dictionnaire de l'Archeologie Chretienne,* now in course of publication, but not, at present, accessible to me.[2]

The ground having been thus cleared by a statement of the proposition which has to be made good, it remains to specify the grounds on which the conclusion rests. This cannot, perhaps, be better done than by reproducing, here, with some additional details, the substance, and for the most part, the very words of an article which appeared in *The Month* just twelve years ago (January, 1902), and which summarized, in the light of Father Cagin's researches published in the meanwhile, the aforesaid contributions to *The Dublin Review.* The argument, it will be observed, is cumulative, and rests on the number of particulars in which the Western rites, notwithstanding differences of detail, show a remarkable agreement among themselves, and a hardly less remarkable divergence from all the Eastern liturgies. Here, then, are the particulars:

1. Throughout the East the liturgical prayers—as distinct from the Scripture lessons and the choral portions of the Mass—are invariable, in this sense, that they do not change from day to day in accordance with the festival or the season. There are, indeed, many different sets of such prayers in use in the East, a number of different "Masses" (*i.e.,* series of Mass-prayers), which bear the names of St. James, St. Mark, St. Chrysostom, St. Basil, and so forth; but the point is that each of these Masses was intended as a fixed form of daily or weekly

---

for the most part on the same considerations, some of which are put forth in his dissertation as entirely new" (Lucas, in *The Month,* Jan. 1902, p. 6). In the article here quoted, Father Cagin's dissertation was erroneously ascribed to Dom A. Mocquereau, the general editor of the *Paleographie Musicale.*

[2] Of this most valuable work I have, for reasons previously stated, been able to utilize only the article on the liturgy of Africa.

service; and any later usage by which different Masses have been assigned to different days must be regarded as entirely distinct in character from the system, common to all the Churches of the West, by which portions of the Mass-prayers were made to vary from day to day in accordance with the ecclesiastical calendar. This contrast has of course been repeatedly noticed by writers on the subject, and may be said to be matter of common knowledge. But the importance of the line of demarcation thus established between all the Western liturgies on the one side and all the Eastern on the other, has been insisted on at considerable length and in detail by Father Cagin.[3]

2. Another particular in which the Western liturgies agree, or can be shown to have originally agreed, as against the Eastern, is, as has been pointed out in a former chapter, that in the formula by which the words of institution are immediately introduced, the Western liturgies without exception have—or formerly had—the words, "Qui pridie (or, Ipse enim pridie) quam pateretur;" whereas the Eastern liturgies, likewise without exception, have, "in qua nocte tradebatur," or an equivalent phrase.[4] This, it will be seen on consideration, is a point of quite primary importance. The agreement, on the one hand and on the other, cannot be accidental; the liturgies which have either the one form or the other must have derived it from some common source, and whereas the Easterns might have derived theirs independently from the text of the New Testament, this is not the case with the form which embodies the words "pridie" and "pateretur"; for neither word occurs in any of the Scriptural narratives of the institution of the Eucharist. Whether, as the "Liber Pontificalis" seems to imply, the Western formula was introduced in Rome by Pope Alexander I (a.d. 108—118), may be regarded as not quite

---

[3] Cagin, pp. 45 ff.

[4] Dublin Review, Oct. 1893, p. 115; Cagin, pp. 55 ff.

Chapter XVI: The Roman and Early Gallican Rite 173

certain, but at any rate it is impossible to suggest any other local origin from which it can be supposed to have spread over the whole of Western Christendom.[5]

Only less important than the "Qui pridie" as a witness to the common origin of the Western liturgies, is the little preface to the Pater noster, and the subsumption or clausula of the same prayer. Every one of the Western liturgies, and not one of the Eastern, has two formulae corresponding, respectively, both in structure and in phraseology, to the "Praeceptis salutaribus" and to the "Libera nos" of the Roman rite. The two cases deserve to be studied separately. Take first the " praefatiuncula."

3. There is, indeed, in all the Eastern liturgies, except the three primitive ones which omit the Lord's Prayer altogether, a prologue which serves to lead up to it, and which is to this extent analogous to the little preface of the Western rites. But in the West the introductory formula is distinguished by two characteristic features, viz., (a) that it is relatively short, and (b) that it normally and almost invariably contains some reference to the divine precept ("Praeceptis salutaribus moniti," &c.). In the Eastern liturgies, on the other hand, the student will, I believe, look in vain for an introductory formula which embodies just this thought.[6] In this connection it may be added that Father Cagin notes a special form of the prologue to the

---

[5] See above, chapter xi. Duchesne is surely mistaken when he writes: "L'auteur attribue ici a Alexandre l'insertion dans la liturgie du Qui pridie, c'est a dire des paroles commemoratives de l'institution de l'eucharistie." There is question here, not of words "commemorative of the institution of the Eucharist," but of inserting in the words commemorative of the institution a phrase commemorative of the passion—that is to say, of substituting "Qui pridie quam pateretur" for "In qua nocte tradebatur." Altaserra's observation, quoted by Duchesne, ad loc., is beside the mark: "Constitutum de memoria passionis Christi in missa celebranda non est proprium Alexandri, sed potius ipsius Christi."

[6] Cf. Brightman, p. 59 (Syrian); 134 f. (Egyptian); 339 (Byzantine); &c.

Pater noster ("Divino magisterio edocti," &c.), formerly prescribed for the Mass of Holy Saturday in the Ambrosian rite, and still allowed on that day as an alternative. This survival from ancient times suggests, on the one hand, that the prologue was once variable in the Ambrosian as well as in the Gallican rite, and on the other hand confirms what has been said as to the close affinity of all Western "praefatiunculae."[7] The single instance which affords a modified or partial exception to the above statement so far as it relates to the Eastern rites is to be found in the liturgy of the Coptic Jacobites, printed by Mr. Brightman from a thirteenth century MS., a witness hardly available for an even relatively early usage, and in agreement neither with the Greek "Liturgy of St. Mark" nor with that of the Abyssinian Jacobites. The text is in fact, quite late enough to have been affected by Roman influences. Yet even in this isolated example the prayer which introduces the Pater noster fills nearly the whole of one of Mr. Brightman's pages; and it is only in the conclusion of the prayer that we read the words which recall the Western formulas, viz., "Bestow upon us Thy Holy Spirit that with a pure heart... we make bold in fearless confidence to say the holy prayer which Thy beloved Son gave ... saying ... pray ye thus, and say: Our Father, &c."[8]

4. Turning now to the embolism ("Libera nos Domine," &c.), we find, indeed, in the liturgy of St. Mark the words: "We beseech Thee, God the Father Almighty, that Thou wouldst not lead us into temptation, but deliver us from evil," and a similar form is found in the Coptic and in the Syrian liturgy of St. James.[9] This is the nearest approach to the Western "Libera," from which, however, it differs by subsuming, first of all, the petition, "lead us not into temptation." In the Byzantine liturgy

---

[7] Cagin, p. 130.

[8] Brightman, pp. 181 f.

[9] Pp. 136, 182, 60.

Chapter XVI: The Roman and Early Gallican Rite 175

the embolism is a prayer to the effect that God would look down in mercy on the bowed heads of the congregation.[10] By contrast with all this, the Western embolism in the great majority of cases begins with the words "Libera nos" ("Deliver us"); and in all but one of the few instances in which this is not so, the general purport of the embolism is the same as that of the Roman form. Thus, the Bobbio Missal has only one such prayer, and this—identical with the Roman—is in the "Missa cottidiana Romensis"; an indication that in the Church for which the Missal was prepared this part of the service was invariable. The Reichenau book has two, each commencing with the word "Libera." The "Missale Gallicanum" has three, two commencing with "Libera," the third with "Exerce Liberator, in nobis juris proprii facultatem,"—an appeal to God as our Deliverer. The "Missale Gothicum" has 17, all except three beginning with "Libera." One (in the 17th Mass) has "Ab omni malo nos eripe" ("Rescue us from all evil"), another (27) has "Exerce Liberator," &c., as in the case cited above, while yet another has in this place a collect "Adesto Domine fidelibus tuis," &c. ("Come, O Lord, to the aid of Thy faithful," &c.), which is obviously out of place, and is in fact identical with one of the collects in the Leonianum.[11] The Mozarabic embolism, according to present usage, is invariable, and begins: "Liberati a malo, confirmati in bono," &c. ("Delivered from evil and strengthened in good," &c.), a form which is plainly in close relationship with the Roman. Moreover, in each of five Celtic liturgical fragments given by Warren, the embolism begins, like the Roman, with the words "Libera nos."[12]

---

[10] Pp. 340, 392, 411.

[11] *The Month*, l.c. p. 9. It ought to have been there mentioned that these particulars, collected independently by the present writer, are likewise given by Cagin, p. 132, where a complete and detailed list of Gallican embolisms is set forth.

[12] Cagin, pp. 132 f. (note).

5. A further point which calls for consideration is this. Although, as a simple matter of counting, the Gallican liturgy can show eleven variables as against five or six which are found in the Roman, yet when the facts of the case are analyzed, the results are found to be very different from those which might have been anticipated from a crude statement of the merely numerical contrast, a contrast, moreover, which tells rather against than in favor of the hypothesis that the Gallican liturgy is to be referred to a distinctively Eastern origin. In the first place, two at least of the eleven Gallican variables answer precisely, as has been shown, to corresponding fixed formulae in the Roman Mass; and the circumstance that these formulae are fixed in the Roman rite is probably due to the same tendency which led St. Gregory to restrict the number of variable prefaces, and of variable clauses in the Canon of the Mass, which previously to his time had been very considerably greater. But more than this. Of the remaining nine variables, six will be found to fall into couples, and this in such a way that each consists, or originally consisted, of an invitatory formula followed by a collect. Moreover, each of the couples thus constituted corresponds to a single Roman or Ambrosian prayer, with its invitatory reduced to the lowest terms in the single word "Oremus." This point must be dealt with somewhat more in detail. The actual facts of the case may perhaps be best indicated by means of a comparative table, substantially identical with one which was originally given in the Dublin Review. The first column shows, in their order, those variable portions of the Gallican liturgy which were in ordinary use. The second and third columns show the corresponding portions of the Mozarabic and the Roman liturgy respectively. For the sake of clearness, the titles of all variables are given in capitals, those of fixed formulae in ordinary type.

Chapter XVI: The Roman and Early Gallican Rite

	Gallican	*Mozarabic*	*Roman*
{	1. PRAEFATIO MISSAE[1]	MISSA.[6]	"OREMUS"
	2. COLLECTIO SEQUENS	ALIA ORATIO	[COLLECT[8]]
	(Recitatio nominum)	(Recitatio Nominum)	

{	3. COLLECTIO POST NOMINA	ORAT. POST. NOMINA.	"ORATE FRATRES" SECRETA.
	4. COLLECTIO AD PACEM[3]	ORATIO AD PACEM.	

{	5. IMMOLATIO MISSAE[4] ("Sanctus")	ILLATIO. ("Sanctus")	PREFACE ("Sanctus")
	6. POST SANCTUS ("Qui Pridie," &c.	POST SANCTUS ["Qui Pridie," &c.][7]	("Te igitur,") &c.[9] ("Qui Pridie," &c.)
	7. POST MYSTERIA.[5]	POST PRIDIE	"Unde et Memores," &c.

{	8. ANTE ORAT. DOMINICAM	AD ORAT. DOM.	"Praeceptis salutaribus," &c.
		(Oratio Dominica)	(Oratio Dominica)
	9. POST ORAT. DOMINICAM	Post Orat. Dom. (Invariable)[11]	"Libera nos," &c.

{	10. POST EUCHARISTIAM.	(Wanting)	"Oremus"
	11. CONSUMMATIO MISSAE.[10]	Oratio (invariable).[12]	POST-COMMUNION.

1. The Gallican "praefatio" is of course by no means to be confounded with the "preface" of the Roman Mass, to which it in no way corresponds. This prayer, or rather invitatory, is often without a title in the Gallican books. Sometimes it is entitled "Collectio." (See the texts in *P.L.* lxxii and in Neale and Forbes, *passim*). In fifty-four instances, in the four Gallican Mass-books taken together, it has retained its true character as an invitatory.

2. The usual rubric is "Collectio sequitur." Sometimes this prayer is called "Collectio ante Nomina."

3. In the *Sacr. Gall,* this prayer is twice called "Collectio super munera" (Nos. 29, 33), and thrice has the rubric "Collectio sequitur" (Nos. 31, 36, 39).

4. Often called "Contestatio."

5. Very often entitled "Post secreta."

6. The Mozarabic "Missa" is always an invitatory formula, never a prayer properly so called.

7. The words "Qui pridie" are not now found in the Mozarabic Mass, as may be seen in *P.L.* lxxxv. 116 and 550. That they were formerly used is, however, unmistakably attested by the title of the following prayer, still called "Post pridie." (*Dublin Review,* pp. 581, 115; Cagin, p. 55.)

8. It has been already pointed out (chap. vii.) that the original position of the Roman collect was after the Gospel, a trace of which usage still survives in the Mass of the Presanctified on Good Friday.

9. The "Te igitur" and "Unde et memores" correspond in position but not in general structure to the Gallican "Post Sanctus" and "Post pridie." See above, chap. x.

10. Five times in the *M. Goth.* (Nos. 4, 6, 8, 11, 12), and seven times in the Sacr. Gall. (Nos. 4, 17, 26-29, 33) this prayer has the rubric "Collectio sequitur." Many Masses have no "proper" post-eucharistic prayers, just as in the Roman Missal many Masses have no "proper" *secreta* or *postcommunion.*

11. Note that, whereas of the two formulae which accompany the *Pater Noster,* both vary in the Gallican, only the first is changed from day to day in the Mozarabic, and neither in the Roman rite.

12. An instructive instance of the way in which an invariable prayer in one rite may precisely answer to a variable prayer in another.

There is perhaps some reason to fear that the foregoing

Chapter XVI: The Roman and Early Gallican Rite   179

table, though clear enough to its compiler, may yet puzzle the reader who approaches the subject for the first time. It may therefore be well to take it piece by piece, and to begin with the middle section (Nos. 5-9), repeating it in an abridged form.

$\left\{\begin{array}{l}\text{5. Immolatio Missae}\\ \text{6. Post Sanctus}\\ \text{7. Post Mysteria.}\end{array}\right.$ | Illatio.
Post Sanctus
Post Pridie | Preface
"Te igitur," &c.
"Unde et Memores," &c.

$\left\{\begin{array}{l}\text{8. Ante Orat.}\\ \text{Dominicam}\\ \text{9. Post Orat.}\\ \text{Dominicam}\end{array}\right.$ | Ad Orat. Dom.
Post Orat. Dom.
(Invariable) | "Praeceptis salutaribus," &c.
(Oratio Dominica)
"Libera nos," &c.

Now it is plain that the Gallican "Immolatio" and the Mozarabic "Illatio" are structurally identical with the Roman Preface, from which they differ only in title and in verbal text. And how closely the prayers "Ante Orationem Dominicam" and "Post Orationem Dominicam" of the Gallican rite correspond, in general purport, with the Roman "Preceptis Salutaribus," &c., and "Libera nos," &c., has already been shown. So much, then, for Nos. 5, 8, and 9 of the table. As regards No. 6, reasons have been given for holding that the Roman "Te igitur," &c., has displaced an earlier "Post Sanctus," similar, at least in general purport, to the Gallican. And lastly, the Gallican "Post Mysteria" (No. 7) usually though not invariably has, like the Roman "Unde et memores," &c., the character of an anamnesis or prayer of remembrance.

Hence the one great structural difference between the Roman and the Gallican rite, as regards the central portion of the Mass, lies in the presence of intercessory prayers in the Roman Canon, and it can, I think, hardly be doubted that in this respect the Gallican arrangement represents an earlier stage in the development of the liturgy. There remain the three couples numbered respectively 1-2 (the Praefatio and Collectio sequens), 3-4 (the C. post Nomina and the C. ad Pacem), and 10-

11 (the post Eucharistiam and the Consummatio Missae). That in a general way the Gallican Collectio sequens (and the Mozarabic Alia Oratio) answers to the Roman collect, the Oratio ad Pacem to the Roman Secreta, and the Consummatio Missae to the Roman Postcommunion, there can be no reasonable doubt. Lest, however, any question should be raised about the relation of the Collectio ad Pacem to the Secreta, I will give here a few specimens of Gallican prayers ad Pacem.

"Suscipe, quaesumus, Domine, *hostiam placationis et laudis*; et has oblationes famulorum famularumque tuarum ... placatus assume."[13]

"Laetificet nos, quaesumus, Domine, *munus oblatum*, ut... tuae sumamus indulgentiae largitatem."[14]

"Suscipe, Domine, preces populi tui *cum oblationibus hostiarum:* ut paschalibus initiati mysteriis, ad aeternitatis ... medelam, te operante, proficiant," &c.[15]

I do not of course pretend that more than a minority of the "Collectiones ad Pacem" are of this type, or that those which are of this type can be regarded as equally primitive in structure with the more numerous collects ad Pacem in which there is an explicit petition for peace; but the unquestionable fact that the old peace- collect gradually became assimilated in character to the Roman secreta, to which (as may be seen in the Bobbio Missal) it finally gave place, appears to me to amount to a clear proof—if indeed any proof were needed—that the prayers corresponded at least in position.[16]

Further, that the Gallican Praefatio Missae, like the Mozarabic "Missa" was, originally, not an independent prayer, but an invitation to pray, prefixed to the first true collect, has

---

[13] *M. Goth.* n. 37.

[14] *Ibid.* n. 56.

[15] *M. Gall.* n. 27.

[16] It has been mentioned above that the "Collectio ad Pacem" occasionally has the title "Super munera."

been pointed out by Mgr. Duchesne, by the present writer in the *Dublin Review,* and lastly by Father Cagin. For the sake of emphasizing the point the following words may be quoted: "A careful examination of the Gallican Masses in the five Sacramentaries reveals the fact that the Praefatio was originally a hortatory address to the people, a 'bidding prayer,' or invitation to pray, and that the collect which immediately follows is the prayer which answers to the invitation. This is indicated by the word 'sequitur,' which in so large a number of instances qualifies the ... collect (i.e., praemissa praefatione collectio sequitur)."[17] So too Father Cagin writes: "La *Praefatio missae* gallicane est generalment une monition aux fideles, une courte invitation a s'orienter dans le sens qu'elle indique, et e'est ce que realise la formule suivante. Le nom Collectio sequitur, donne a sette formule, semble choisi a dessein pour exprimer formellement sa relation avec la Praefatio missae.[18]

That the "Post Eucharistiam" holds a like relation to the "Consummatio Missae" has also been noticed by the same three writers, and there is, indeed, no difficulty in verifying the statement.

But it is strange that neither Mgr. Duchesne nor Father Cagin should have observed that precisely the same thing is true of the "Collectio post Nomina" and the "Collectio ad Pacem." In the Reichenau Mass-book, which is the most archaic specimen of its class, out of six "collectiones post nomina," no less than five have the invitatory form.[19] In the Missale Gothicum, out of sixty-nine Masses which admit of comparison, twenty-one have a "collectio post nomina" in this same form.[20] The Gallicanum has four, and the Bobbio Missal six instances

---

[17] *Dublin Review,* l.c. pp. 582, 583 abridged. The writer was mistaken in saying that the fact had been "not hitherto noticed," for it had been very clearly stated by M. Duchesne (Origines, pp. 197 f.).

[18] Cagin, p. 54.

[19] Nos. 2, 3, 6, 8, 11.

[20] These instances are too numerous to be cited in detail.

of similar "collectiones post nomina."[21] The proportion, indeed, is not so large as in the case of the "praefatio Missae" and of the "post Eucharistiam."[22] But the facts show clearly that there was a strong tendency for such prefatory formulae to pass into simple prayers,—mere duplicates, so to say, of the collects which they had originally served to introduce. And although no one could have predicted on *a priori* grounds that it would be so, there is nothing to excite surprise in the circumstance that this tendency seems to have operated sooner in the case of the "collectio post nomina" than in that of the "praefatio Missae" or of the "post Eucharistiam." That the "post nomina" was in fact the first of the three prefatory prayers to lose its prefatory character, appears not merely from the fact that it has retained this character in a relatively smaller number of extant instances, but from the still more significant fact that, in his treatise, "De Officiis," St. Isidore speaks of it as an independent prayer, whereas he recognizes the "praefatio Missae" as a true bidding prayer or invitatory.[23] In his time, therefore, the former had lost, while the latter still retained, its prefatory function.

There is, however, something more to be said before leaving this part of the subject. It has been already asserted that "in a general way" the Gallican "collectio sequens" answers to the first or principal collect of the Roman Mass. To speak more precisely, it answers to it in two particulars, *(a)* as being the chief collect of the Mass, and *(b)* as holding the first place among the variable prayers properly so-called, *i.e.*, as distinct

---

[21] M. Gall. Nos. 1, 26, 35, 39; M. Bobb. Nos. 8, 10, 15, 36, 52, 54.

[22] Of post-eucharistic prayers which have the prefatory form, there are fourteen in the four Gallican books taken together. Of "post nomina" which have the same form, there are 37. But the total number of collects "post nomina" is much larger (133) than that of collects "post Eucharistiam" (27).

[23] Of the "Missa," he says: "Prima oratio *admonitionis* est erga populum, ut excitemur ad exorandum Deum," but of the "Oratio ad Pacem" he writes: "Quarta post haec infertur pro osculo pacis, ut charitate reconciliati," &c. (*De Officiis*, i. 15; *Dublin Review*, p. 580.)

Chapter XVI: The Roman and Early Gallican Rite 183

from mere invitations to pray. To this may be added the circumstance that a considerable number of Gallican "collectiones sequentes" are verbally, or all but verbally, identical with Roman collects. The position, however, of the Gallican "collectio sequens" was, as has been said, not that which the Roman collect now holds. For, together of course with its invitatory, it followed the Gospel. But reasons have been given, in Chapters vii. and viii., for believing that the position of the chief collect in the Roman Mass has been altered, and that it, too, originally followed the Gospel. "A curious and instructive instance of this transfer having actually been made is found in the 'Missa Ecclesiae Romanae' of the Stowe Missal, when compared with the 'Cottidiana Romensis' of the Bobbio Mass-book. The Bobbio Mass embodies the Roman Canon in a thoroughly Gallican framework, with its full complement of collects in their Gallican position. Now, every one of these prayers is found also in the first Mass of the Stowe Missal, but with this difference—that the two first collects (i.e., one which in the Gallican Ordo ought to be a praefatio or bidding prayer, and the collectio sequens) appear in the Stowe Missal in the Roman position, before the Scripture lessons."[24]

In conclusion a reflection may be permitted on the ultimate suppression, or supersession, partly under papal but partly also under imperial influence, of the early Gallican rite in favor of the Roman, a change which some Anglican writers have seen fit to deplore. The following paragraphs were, in substance, written many years ago, and there seems to be no good reason for modifying them except in the way of a slight curtailment.[25]

1. No one who has not carefully examined for himself the early Gallican sacramentaries can have any adequate idea of the extraordinary want of uniformity which they present. It

---

[24] *Dublin Review*, Oct. 1893, p. 585. For the sake of clearness I have made one or two slight verbal corrections in the above passage.

[25] *Dublin Review*, Jan. 1894, pp. 129 ff.

must be enough to say that out of about 175 Masses which the six Missals (including the Stowe Missal) contain, there are not three which are common to any two of the books. Indeed, it would seem that the only Mass which really had a kind of fixed identity was the "Missa cottidiana Romensis," which appears in the Bobbio and in the Stowe Missals, and of which a fragment has survived in the "M. Gothicum."

2. Not less remarkable than the want of uniformity among the Gallican books themselves, is the fact that a very large proportion of the variable prayers which they contain are found also in the Roman sacramentaries, from which even Neale and Forbes admit that they must have been for the most part borrowed. Moreover, with the exception of the fragmentary Reichenau Missal, every one of the other books contains evidence of the occasional use of the Roman Canon, or of portions thereof. Indeed, nothing can be more clear than that long before the time of Pepin and Charlemagne the Roman rite had begun to obtain a firm footing in Gaul.[26]

Here then was a state of things in the Gallican Church which manifestly clamored for a reform, and what reform could have been more reasonable than to substitute for the unstable and undeveloped liturgical system of Gaul the fixed and clear-cut Roman rite with its fully developed calendar of seasons and festivals?

Nevertheless, nothing can be more clear than that this reform was not thrust upon the Gallican Church by the Roman Pontiffs.[27] The very substitution of the Roman for the old Gallican rite was gradually effected throughout the West, with the cordial co-operation, indeed, of the Roman pontiffs, but by

---

[26] This truth has been set forth in the clearest light by Dom S. Baumer in his study of the Gelasianum. It would be impossible here to indicate the fresh evidence by which he proves to demonstration the strong influence of the Roman rite in Gaul in the sixth, seventh, and eighth centuries.

[27] Marchesi, *La Liturgia Gallicana* (Rome, 1867), ii. 205 ff.; Baumer, *Sacr. Gelas*, pp. 49 ff.

no means at their unduly urgent request.

For any trace of an attempt on the part of the Popes to suppress with a high hand the ancient Gallican liturgy we seek in vain.[28]

4. It was not until the eleventh century that the substitution of the Roman for the older local liturgy (substantially identical with the Gallican) was effected in Spain. The story of the substitution is a complicated one and cannot be attempted here.[29] But two points stand out clearly when the documents are dispassionately examined—viz., (a) that the Roman See was prepared to defend the cause of the Spanish liturgy when it was unjustly attacked on dogmatic grounds; and (b) that it was not until the Roman rite had gained a footing in Spain, and was supported by a strong party in Aragon and Castile, that Gregory VII authoritatively urged its universal adoption. It is, of course, easy to ascribe this action of St. Gregory to "that intolerance of other rites," which—in the words of an Anglican writer—has so incalculably "injured ecclesiastical antiquity." It would perhaps be wiser as well as more modest, if only in view of the moderation of earlier Pontiffs, to give even Pope Hildebrand credit for some other motive than a spirit of narrow-minded exclusiveness or tyrannical intolerance. There were, after all, more important interests at stake than the preservation of interesting liturgical relics for the satisfaction of students in centuries to come. We must not judge of the condition of the Spanish liturgy solely by the Mozarabic Missal in the form in which it has come down to us from the time of Cardinal Ximenes. Had such a Missal been in universal use in Spain, we may confidently assume that St. Gregory VII would have left it in undisturbed possession. But liturgical chaos was quite another matter. And were we in possession of all the

---

[28] On the gradual supersession of the Gallican rite see Fortescue, pp. 177 ff.

[29] The chief authorities are (1) *Regesta Gregorii* VII. in *P.L.* cxlviii.; (2) Pien (Pinius) *De Liturgia Mozarabica* in the Bollandist *Acta SS.* (Julii, vi. 1-112); (3) Gams, *Kirchengeschichte von Spanien*, ii. 441-462.

circumstances we should probably find ourselves compelled to admit that for this state of chaos the adoption of the Roman rite was the only remedy. How far from the mind of the Roman See is the undiscriminating suppression of "other rites" may be gathered from the measures taken by Pius IX and by Leo XIII for the preservation of the local liturgical usages of the Basilian monastery of Grotta Ferrata, hardly a dozen miles from Rome.

THE END

More Titles available from Mediatrix Press!

The All Soul's Forget-me-not

The Autobiography of St. Charles of Sezze

Capuchin Chronicle

Commentary for Oblates on the Rule of St. Benedict

Defence of the Priesthood by St. John Fisher

Elizabeth Canori Mora: Wife, Mother and Mystic

Fr. Simeon Lourdel: Planting the Faith in the furthest Africa

Mariology in 3 vols. Edited by Fr. Juniper Carol, O.F.M.

Moral Theology by St. Alphonsus Liguori

Pious Union of St. Joseph

Public Life of Our Lord Jesus Christ

Purgatory, by St. Robert Bellarmine

Rome and the Counter-Reformation in England

St. John Fisher

St. Thomas More: A Great Man in Hard Times

Spiritual Life of Cardinal Merry del Val

True Story of the Sword in the Stone: The life of St. Galgano

For these and other great titles, visit us at:
www.mediatrixpress.com

www.ingramcontent.com/pod-product-compliance
Lightning Source LLC
Chambersburg PA
CBHW011130070526
44583CB00023B/2971